Marriage is a land of unpredictable seasons, where springtime can turn wintry in a heartbeat. It's rife with hail storms, flash floods, cold snaps, heat waves, most without warning. How do we not just survive it, but learn to bear fruit at all times? Deane Schuessler is a kind of weatherman of the heart, and more: a wise, gentle and skillful field guide who has learned the art of life together. Here he teaches us the secrets of that art.

MARK BUCHANAN,
author of *The Holy Wild* and *The Rest of God*

St. Paul boldly compared the relationship of husband and wife to that of Christ and the Church. Pastor, missionary, husband, father, and grandfather Deane Schuessler takes the analogy seriously and vividly explores the gracious possibilities God holds for marriage. Having been married for over forty years myself but working with many newlyweds at Concordia, I appreciated Deane's efforts to speak to marriages in both the early and mature years of marriage. Although roughly half the book is devoted to each age group, the devotions show how God's gracious possibilities for marriage apply, in some sense, to all marriages. The combination of biblical references with pastoral experience will, by God's grace, leave marriage partners closer to God and each other. Marriage partners will praise God and thank Deane for this inspiring labor of love.

DR. ROBERT HOLST,
President of Concordia University, St. Paul, MN

Devoted to God and Each Other brings it all together for couples who want to invite God into their marriage—Bible, prayer, experience, and life application. With a warm, pastoral spirit, like a friend speaking the truth in love, Deane Schuessler offers a gentle guide for living, no, thriving through the seasons of marriage. There is teaching going on here, but more, the whisper of wisdom from a servant in touch with the heart of God.

REV. DR. DEAN NADASDY,
Senior Pastor, Woodbury Lutheran Church (MN)

DEVOTED TO
GOD
and
EACH OTHER

DEVOTED TO
GOD
a n d
EACH OTHER

To Jim + Peg, faithful to our Lord, and Faithful in His work, Stay devoted!

Deane Schuessler

DEANE
SCHUESSLER

WINEPRESS WP PUBLISHING

Unless otherwise noted, all Scriptures are taken from the Holy Bible, New Living Translation, copyright © 1996 by Tyndale Charitable Trust. Used by permission of Tyndale House Publishers, Wheaton, Illinois 60189. All rights reserved.

Scripture references marked NIV are taken from the Holy Bible, New International Version, Copyright © 1973, 1978, 1984 by the International Bible Society. Used by permission of Zondervan Publishing House. The "NIV" and "New International Version" trademarks are registered in the United States Patent and Trademark Office by International Bible Society.

Scripture references marked KJV are taken from the King James Version of the Bible.

Scripture references marked TMB are taken from The Message Bible © 1993 by Eugene N. Peterson, NavPress, PO 35001, Colorado Springs, CO 80935, 4th printing in USA 1994. Published in association with the literary agency—Aline Comm. PO 49068, Colorado Springs, CO 80949. Used by permission.

ISBN 1-57921-837-7
Library of Congress Catalog Card Number: 2006900982

DEDICATION

To Julie, my beloved, God-given wife:
Your love has taught me more about
healthy marriage than I could learn
from many books and counseling
many couples . . . and has enabled
the writing of this book.

TABLE OF CONTENTS

PART

1

DEVOTIONS FOR
THE EARLY YEARS OF
MARRIAGE

INTRODUCTION

I t was a scented Honolulu evening—I love the fragrance of jasmine bushes. My phone rang. The young husband of one year pleaded through my receiver: "Could you come over to our apartment right away? Jenny's* heading for the door. Says she's leaving." Across the lines, I heard the panic in his voice.

"I'll be right over," I said.

Driving the car to my first marriage counseling session-on-the-run, I wondered what they would say; what I could say. A fresh-spanking pastoral intern of two months, I had no idea how I would handle my first counseling crisis. Jenny stood by their opened apartment door, keys in hand. "I need some air," she announced.

Greg* addressed Jenny, "Let's ask Pastor Deane to drive. We're too upset." I drove, while Jenny and Greg sat in the back. Greg was almost beside himself with entreaty. His next words are forever lodged in my memory: "Jenny . . . Jenny . . . I love you . . . I love you *more than God himself.*" I had to bite my lip to prevent explosive words from spraying out. He said he loved Jenny more than he loved God himself? He would be willing to make an idol of his wife. Jenny instinctively realized that was precisely her husband's problem. Greg looked to his wife to fill his deepest needs and fears—needs only God could fill, fears only God could quell.

* Not real names.

Out of the frantic *void* that left only fear in its wake, Greg wildly claimed he loved his wife. He stood poised over the gaping quarry of his void, trying to fill it with empty air words. The void in his heart remained. This book is about filling voids in your heart, in your marriage. Whatever fills your voids—words of life, love and health, or words of emptiness and death—will determine the condition of your marriage.

When God grants us to be married, he links together our two most vital relationships: with *him*—the deepest, most important of all—and our relationship with our *spouse*—the most intimate of human relationships. What happens in the one relationship will impact the quality of the other relationship. The two relationships are inextricably combined. That is why my wife Julie chose the title for this book: *Devoted to God and Each Other.*

As our devotion to God grows, our trust in each other deepens. As we trust, we love each other with more confidence and less fear, with greater joy and less hesitancy. God grants us the ability to love with greater sincerity and freedom. And yes, with greater passion.

These devotions grew out of many years of marriage with Julie and many years of pastoral ministry. The first 15 of those years we served as missionaries in northern Japan. I was director and pastor of the Sapporo Youth Center and Congregation. I worked with young people and performed many of their weddings. During the subsequent years, I've been serving in Minnesota's Twin Cities metroplex. My work with couples continues to this day. And I love this service.

A recurring theme throughout these devotions is: When God grants us to be married, he gives us a great gift. When we accept each other as the huge gifts from God we are, he enables us to perceive our life together as a true privilege, not a drag. Willingness and joy form great soil in which marital love sprouts and grows. Voids shrink, and the seed of God's loving life takes root and blossoms.

God granted Julie and me three children and ten grandchildren. Has our life been stimulating? Every once in a while she says, "I could do with a little more quiet, even a bit of boredom." But we wouldn't trade our lives. May love and care for each other, sprouting from God's Word, nourish your marriage.

God bless you richly as you read the devotions, work on the **Let's apply** brief practice activities, and pray the petitions in **Let's pray together.**

These devotions are divided in two: Part 1 provides devotions for you couples who are in the early years of marriage, while Part 2 is for you who are in your mature years. These two eras form the bookends of our married lives; between them our middle years are suspended. During those middle years, we look back to the early years to keep the first fires of enthusiasm burning. At the same time we look ahead to our mature years, hoping to finish strong in our lives with our spouses. Thus in all three periods of our married lives we will, God willing, be sufficiently motivated and inspired in Christ.

"You Are the Wind Beneath My Wings" is sung at many weddings and receptions. Humbly I would alter the interpretation to say God is the ultimate "wind beneath our wings." He assures us of his love for us, filling our deepest void. Paul wrote, "You have been given fullness in Christ" (Colossians 2:9). *Then,* as agents of God's love, he uses us as marital partners to give buoyancy and lift to help keep each other afloat.

May the power and aroma of God's love fill your voids and permeate your marriage. May he enhance you with joy like fragrant jasmine—or whatever your favorite aroma may be.

CHAPTER 1

FLAMBOYANT JOY

Then you will sing psalms and hymns and spiritual songs among yourselves, making music to the Lord in your hearts. And you will always give thanks for everything to God the Father in the name of the Lord Jesus Christ.

—Ephesians 5:19–20

Weddings, music, and laughter form a trio of joy. In all the weddings I've performed over the years, all but one had hearty ingredients of music. That one exception reminded me strangely of a funeral. Music was missing.

The rest of the weddings included music, lots of it. The caption of Psalm 45 designates it as "a wedding song." The music in the wedding worship service is full of joy, as we lift our hearts to praise God, and as we offer our sincere prayers for the Lord to bless the bride and groom. Christian wedding music is lovely and noble in spirit, full of beauty and inspiration. It is the music of faith and love—not just human love, but God's own love, which we pray will reverberate in the new couple's hearts and home.

Music at wedding receptions rings with happiness, romance, and rhythm. Our toes start tapping. Soon our legs take us out on the dance floor. Some love to dance, others vicariously enjoy watching friends and relatives smile and swing to the music.

Think of the people who came to your wedding. There were the solid, dignified relatives, whose very presence announced: "This in an *important* occasion." Then in walked Cousin Fred, the one with the knack for revving up the crowd, dropping the unexpected quip, laughing in the way that sets others laughing with him. Laughter is part of the music of weddings. As William Makepeace Thackeray said, "A good laugh is sunshine in the house." Thank God for our Flamboyant Freddies.

What would weddings be without laughter? And music? God's Word, prayer, music, good food, appropriate humor, and music lift our spirits out of the humdrum into motions of joy.

Let's apply: Discuss with each other what concerns or fears might block you from expressing your joy as a couple. Ask God to help you move off dead centers of anxiety and into the momentum of joy, trimming your worries down to manageable size where they belong.

Let's pray together: Dear Lord God, you are the source of all our joy and sense of fulfillment. Help us shake off sadness and the stifling sin of worry. Renew us with fresh reasons to rejoice. We need the lift of your joy, O God, whether it's spoken, sung, or laughed. "The joy of the Lord is your strength" (Nehemiah 8:10). Amen.

CHAPTER 2

FREE FOR

ONE FULL YEAR

A newly married man must not be drafted into the army or given any other special responsibilities. He must be free to be at home for one year, bringing happiness to the wife he has married.

—Deuteronomy 24:5

Do you believe what you just read? To us in this fast-paced 21st century, this Old Testament custom may seem like an unheard-of *luxury of time*.

To allow the husband to spend as much time with his newlywed wife as possible, God's Word exempted him from serving in the army, or having any other special responsibilities to the larger community for a whole year. The couple's extended family and neighbors picked up the slack.

God knows that we husbands and wives need unhurried time to be with each other, especially after we've just married. We need time to talk and get to know each other. We need time to tell our stories and share our experiences . . . experiences from childhood, thoughts about our successes and failures, dreams for the future, and what God is currently doing in our lives. That's why God ordered that special allowance be made for newlyweds to have quality time together during their first year of marriage.

One of the reasons it may be hard to "love one another and work together with one heart and purpose" (Philippians 2:2) is that we haven't gotten to know each other well. Often the bugaboo is busyness. Nowadays many couples both work. With so many responsibilities outside the home, we find it difficult to lasso quiet "down time" hours to be home with each other.

When God created marriage, he intended for us emotionally to "leave . . . father and mother and be united to [our] wife/husband, and . . . become one flesh" (Genesis 2:24). We need to make a clear transition *from* loyalty to our biological family *to* loyalty to our wife/husband. To complete the transition, we need unrushed time together soon after marriage.

Let's apply: How can you work out your schedules so you can have supper together as often as possible? Put into your regular schedule a weekly date night. If that first year of your marriage has already passed, how can you maximize the time you spend together from now on?

Let's pray together: Lord, you know what each moment is best used for. Please help us slow our pace so we can spend unhurried time together. Help us savor this prime time. Help us become one in spirit, in purpose, *in you!* In Christ we pray. Amen.

CHAPTER 3

MARRYING THE

WHOLE FAMILY

Ruth replied, "Don't ask me to leave you and turn back. I will go wherever you go and live wherever you live. Your people will be my people, and your God will be my God."

—Ruth 1:16

Congratulations on your wedding! And congratulations on becoming part of a new extended family. For, "When you get married, you marry the whole family." Getting to know your new set of relatives may not happen quickly or easily.

Sometimes working through issues with your new extended family may seem like an unfair burden. But if your relationship with your husband or wife's family is positive, you will find them a real asset to yourself and your family.

That's how it worked for Naomi and Ruth, who hailed from two different countries. After both their husbands died, mother-in-law Naomi and daughter-in-law Ruth found they had more than their loneliness in common. A strong spiritual connection began to develop, which Ruth was the first to notice. Not long after they became widows, Naomi assumed Ruth would return to her family and homeland in Moab. But Ruth surprised her mother-in-law by asking permission to return with her to Israel. Having seen the light of God, his love and truth, shining through Naomi, Ruth came to believe in Naomi's *God:* "Your God will be my God."

We are touched by the depth and tenderness of their relationship, but that relationship also took on major historical importance. Ruth is our ancestress by faith: Ruth became the grandmother of King David, and it was from David's ancestral line that Jesus, our Savior and Lord, was born.

Here are two suggestions to help not only to avoid conflicts, but to also develop a loving and trustful relationship with your in-laws:

1. **Communicate with your in-laws.** Whenever there is an issue involving both you and your in-laws—one that could become even remotely touchy—first run your ideas past your husband or wife. Your spouse knows his or her family's favorite words and problem-solving techniques, while you are the "new kid on the block" with much to learn about them. Let your spouse serve as the communication conduit between them and yourself. This will help you avoid a myriad of misunderstandings and hard feelings.

2. **Pray for your in-laws.** Ask your dear Lord to strengthen and help your in-laws in all areas of their lives. Rather than praying for them merely to agree with you, pray for them in their own right, according to their real needs. More than anything else, your prayers will change *your* heart, so that more and more you will think of them the way God thinks of them, and your love for them will grow.

Let's apply: Enumerate the things you have in common with your in-laws, such as faith, values, geography, interests, vocations, and ways of looking at life. Above all, you have their son/daughter in common. During the first years of your marriage, you will probably act extra politely and courteously toward them. As the years increase, you will feel more and more relaxed with them.

Let's pray together: O Lord God, you have given to my beloved wife/husband so much grace through her/his family. Please help me to understand my spouse in the context of his/her family. Help me to appreciate their positive qualities and thank you for them, dear Father. Preserve us from conflicts. Guide our words so we can build healthy relationships, not just as "in-laws." Amen.

CHAPTER 4

IN CHRIST, GOD DOESN'T COUNT OUR SINS

All this newness of life is from God, who brought us back to himself through what Christ did . . . For God was in Christ, reconciling the world to himself, no longer counting people's sins against them.
—2 Corinthians 5:18–19

Y ou received many beautiful wedding gifts. You started your new life together with a whole new set of tools for living. Think about the new beginning you embarked on. Not only did your spouse embrace you, but God also embraced you with his love. God offered both of you a new beginning.

When a certain man was struggling about whether to believe in Christ, he said, "It seems too good to be true, that I'm really forgiven." To our rational minds, it may seem too good to be true that God forgives us freely without our deserving it. That's when faith really moves into action. By faith we "see" that Jesus died on the cross as our substitute. Because of Christ, God does not "count our sins against us."

Jesus sacrificed himself to atone for your sins. He said, "Freely you have received, freely give" (Matthew 10:8). When Jesus gave his life for you, his gift made it possible for two important things to happen: 1) Through his love, both of you now live a new life in his name. 2) God enables you to pass on to each other the rich love you've received from

Jesus. Living with each other you have daily opportunities to practice sharing forgiveness. That's the "gift that keeps on giving."

Let's apply: Review the fact that since God has forgiven you so completely, you can't help but forgive each other—and others you may have conflict with. Read together Jesus' parable in Matthew 18:21–35, about the servant who had been forgiven a huge debt by his master. That servant held a very small I.O.U. from another servant, but was not willing to forgive him. Having started a new life together in marriage, prepare to share that gift of forgiveness as often as necessary.

Let's pray together: Thank you, heavenly Father, for forgiving our past, present, and future sins. Your forgiveness makes us new persons in Christ. Amen.

CHAPTER 5

NEW LIFE . . .
NEW STRENGTH

Don't be afraid, for I am with you. Do not be dismayed, for I am
your God. I will strengthen you. I will help you. I will uphold you
with my victorious right hand.

—Isaiah 41:10

We couples live in the midst of a great deal of uncertainty and insecurity. At times we struggle with fear. Yet by his grace, God allowed us to be partnered in marriage, providing us with a foundation of security for living.

It all began when God caused each of us to be born into our biological family, our family of origin. Then, as we grew up and got married, God enabled us to establish our own family, our nuclear family. It is now our point of reference, our place of refuge when we're buffeted by life's stresses. God is our Creator, Redeemer, Sustainer, the One who fortifies our faith. It is God who is the center, the heartbeat and fulcrum of our life together. He is our Protector, the One who provides for all our needs. He supplies us and our families with strength and support, giving us the guidance we need and the love we crave.

Consider Noah and his family. The world around them had become degenerate. Though living in those surroundings, "Noah was a righteous man, blameless among the people of his time, and he walked with God"

(Genesis 6:9). God blessed Noah and his wife's marriage, and their three sons, Shem, Ham, and Japheth, assisted in building the ark according to God's direction. We can only imagine the stresses they endured from the community around them. God made good on his promise to provide their security: "I will strengthen you. I will help you. I will uphold you with my victorious right hand" (Isaiah 41:10).

Our marriages and families become strong as we share our common source of spiritual nourishment, God's Word and promises.

Let's apply: Tell each other the story of a time growing up when you faced a tough struggle as a family. Where did your power to survive come from?

Let's pray together: O Lord, what a wonderful haven you provided when you allowed us to be married. It is your Word which binds and sustains us, in Christ. Amen.

CHAPTER 6

DO I HAVE TO
WASH AGAIN?

If we confess our sins to him, he is faithful and just to forgive us and
to cleanse us from every wrong.

—1 John 1:9

Martin Luther once said that Christians need to repent every day, as part of their lifestyle. Don't believe the caricature of a person who repents as moping around with a sense of low self-esteem. The opposite is true: we repent as we need to—whenever a wrongdoing is brought to our attention. This results in our staying healthy spiritually, as God rebuilds our joy, confidence, and self-esteem on a daily basis.

We may hesitate to repent. In not wanting to apologize to God, we may be like children whose parents call them in to wash their hands for supper. They protest: "Do we have to wash *again?*"

Admitting we've been wrong stings our pride. Nevertheless God's Holy Spirit makes it possible for us to repent, helping us to recall that Jesus grants us the gift of new life. Once the words "I'm sorry" leave our lips, a broad sense of relief and freedom replaces our fear and pain. Married people who repent to God and apologize to each other, solve their problems more quickly.

Let's apply: Memorize these words, first to yourself, then say them aloud together: "I have been crucified with Christ. I myself no longer live, but Christ lives in me. So I live my life in this earthly body by trusting in the Son of God, who loved me and gave himself for me" (Galatians 2:20). See if this doesn't help build your confidence that when you ask for forgiveness, you truly receive it. You are forgiven and cleansed.

Let's pray together: Thank you, gracious Lord, for accepting us again today. We're grateful that for Jesus' sake you don't count our sins against us. Amen.

CHAPTER 7

DYING TO BE
PRODUCTIVE

I tell you the truth, unless a kernel of wheat falls to the ground and dies, it remains only a single seed. But if it dies, it produces many seeds.

—John 12:24

As marriage partners, every time we wait upon each other's needs we experience a "dying to self," that is, to our sinful tendencies. This is a wholesome dying that is a necessary prerequisite to our spiritual rising again to new life in Christ. In order to fill the important needs of our spouse at a particular time, we put our own ego needs on hold. We patiently work on the immediate issue—whether it's an illness, finances, or a child's problem at school—until it's resolved. That's not easy. Our "flesh" may protest: "When will it be my turn to be the focus of attention and care?"

God wants us to be productive in each arena of our lives, whether in our family, at our job, or whatever it may be. Just as this year's seeds produce next year's crop, this moment's patience plants seeds for our future growth and maturity. So it is with growing a marriage and raising a family. The strength, love, and reliability we muster today form powerful preparations for future growth. In a healthy home, we help each other develop "roots to grow and wings to fly."

It may take a while before we receive recognition from our spouse. Proverbs 31:29 says of the faithful wife: "Her husband . . . praises her: 'Many women do noble things, but you surpass them all.'"

Our process of growth (spiritual dying and rising, repeated as necessary) may feel bothersome and bumpy. Yet each time we survive a crisis, we mark a new step of growth that strengthens us for tomorrow.

Let's apply: When was the last time you survived "one of those times?" Ask yourselves: "Did we grow through that sequence of events? What did we learn that increased our skills in meeting future challenges?

Let's pray together: Help us, gracious Lord, to remember the blessings you funneled to us through previous challenges—blessings that are benefitting us as we live under you today. In the name of Jesus who experienced it all for us, loving us enough to sacrifice his very life for our present and eternal well-being. Amen.

CHAPTER 8

FAITH = BELIEVING TOGETHER

I'm eager to encourage you in your faith, but I also want to be encouraged by yours. In this way, each of us will be a blessing to the other.
—Romans 1:12

We tend to think of believing as a solo action. Some married couples seem to live separate spiritual lives. "You can't believe for someone else; everyone has to believe for him or herself," we hear. That's one side of the coin. The other side is that we are also nourished as we draw upon the same source of help from God.

When we believe together—that is, when both of us exercise our faith at the same time—we function as a believing unit, and are bonded together by our loving God. He creates the kind of faith in us that is alive and active. He cheers us on as we apply faith in the struggles, joys, sorrows, and victories of life.

When we glue a piece of furniture, we use wood clamps to hold the parts together. Like the two sides of the clamp, we husbands and wives can hold tightly to God in faith and love. "Love never gives up, never loses faith, is always hopeful, and endures through every circumstance" (1 Corinthians 13:7).

Trust God jointly as wife and husband. Peter described your role as mutually believing marital partners:

> You are . . . heirs (together) of the gracious gift of life, so that nothing will hinder your prayers.
>
> —1 Peter 3:7

When we believe together, our bond with each other becomes stronger and more capable of carrying a substantial "payload" of responsibility toward each other and our family.

Let's apply: Mention a project that you worked on together as a couple, one that turned out well. What did each of you contribute toward that good outcome? How did your believing together enhance the resolution?

Let's pray together: O Lord, please enable us individually and as a couple to trust you and your reliable promises. Show us how to stimulate and encourage each other in faith. We pray in the power of the Holy Spirit, whom Jesus sends to strengthen us. Amen.

CHAPTER 9

HOPE DOESN'T DISAPPOINT US

Because of our faith, Christ has brought us into this place of highest privilege where we now stand, and we confidently and joyfully look forward to sharing God's glory. . . . And this expectation (hope) will not disappoint us. For we know he has given us the Holy Spirit to fill our hearts with his love.

—Romans 5:2,5

Sometimes you see it in the faces of just-married couples. Sometimes it shows in the calm, smiling mellowness of some middle-aged couples. It's that special by-product of love: that powerful sense of anticipation, which the Bible calls *hope*. Hope is faith settled in for the long haul. Hope is faith aimed forward, hitching the present to the future. Hope is faith extended to the hundredth power, to infinity, to eternity. Hope says, "I'll never give up trusting God." Faith + anticipation = hope.

The worldly counterfeit of hope is luck. Luck is fantasy thinking focused on material things. Eventually luck *will* disappoint us. Trying to solve our problems with luck is trying to nickel-and-dime our way through life instead of living with real hope which God freely provides.

Hope that looks to God will never disappoint us. It keeps going and going, like the Energizer bunny with the batteries in its back. "You are the God who saves me. All day long I put my hope in you" (Psalm 25:5). We grow in hope by spiritually holding onto Christ, who died for us and rose again three days later. Hope keeps us youthful and growing.

We married people need a lot of hearty, healthy hope. When God fulfills a promise for us, we remember it. Solomon was right: "Hope deferred makes the heart sick, but when dreams come true, there is life and joy" (Proverbs 13:12). In the passage above, Romans 5:5, Paul graphically describes hope as a resource that God combines with love. Love and hope are a winning combination.

Filled with hope, we maintain a sturdy, resilient spirit. Hope does wonders for any marriage.

Let's apply: Recall a time when your partner said or did something that caused you to regain your sense of hope and anticipation.

Let's pray together: Dear Lord, when our hopes begin to sag, please refill our reservoir of anticipation. Our sense of anticipation grows out of your powerful promises. Amen.

CHAPTER 10

LOVE MULTIPLIES JOY

You have been called to live in freedom—not freedom to satisfy your sinful nature, but freedom to serve one another in love.
—Galatians 5:13

Choosing a gift that truly gives another person joy is not easy. At times, when we're close to the wire of decision about which gift to give, it can be maddening. We ask ourselves, *What does he or she need* at this time?

The love we feel toward him or her is what motivates and keeps us going until we've made our decision, bought our gift, and have it in hand.

Listen to a person who receives a well thought-through gift: "You've put a great deal of thought into choosing *this gift*. You really thought about me, what I need and what makes me happy. I opened your gift and . . . it's perfect for me! I would have appreciated whatever you gave me, but this gift!"

Giving an appropriate gift to another person resembles giving a fitting compliment. The effect it produces is twofold: it creates *joy*, and it also *rests* him or her emotionally and spiritually. It resolves confusion and helps answer questions like, *How do I stand in his eyes? Am I fulfilling her needs? Am I loving her well?*

A carefully chosen gift not only enhances our love but also multiplies our joy.

Let's apply: *Who you are* takes precedence over *what you give.* But what you give reveals valuable information about who you are in relation to your partner. Think of a gift your partner has given you, one that was especially appropriate, and which revealed significant facts about your relationship. Put your thanks into words.

Let's pray together: Lord God our Father, we worship you way beyond the gifts you give us. Help us think of each other not only for what we do for each other, but of him or her as a person. Ultimately, all gifts come from you. Help us be effective conveyors of your love. Help us maintain and enhance each other's joy. In Jesus, the complete gift-giver. Amen.

CHAPTER 11

PEACE — A QUALITY THAT ATTRACTS

> When the Holy Spirit controls our lives, he will produce this kind of fruit in us: love, joy, peace, patience, kindness, goodness, faithfulness, gentleness, and self-control. Here there is no conflict with the law.
> —Galatians 5:22–23

In the 1960s Vietnam era, the symbol of the peace movement was the dove.

Most Americans think the dove symbol was a product of that era. Actually it goes back thousands of years, to the time of Noah and the ark. After the deluge of rain stopped, Noah waited some months for the waters to recede, evaporate, and settle in the lowlands. Noah released a dove to see if it would return, indicating that the water had not receded enough so the patriarch and his family could safely leave the ark.

The first time, the dove returned. The next time it did not. It *was* safe to leave! What an immense relief when not only Noah and his family, but also the horde of animals and birds could finally leave that smelly ark. The absence of the dove meant "You may now return to normal." How sweet that first piece of fresh fruit tasted in Noah's mouth, and for his wife, three sons and three daughters-in-law.

Then, 2,000 years ago, a dove appeared again, as Matthew reported: "As soon as Jesus was baptized, he went up out of the water. At that moment heaven was opened, and he saw the Spirit of God descending like a dove and alighting on him" (Matthew 3:16). By the dove of the Holy Spirit, God spoke the peace of his approval over his Son Jesus. The Father also spoke his word of approving peace: "This is my Son, whom I love; with him I am well pleased" (verse 17).

When was the last time you and your husband or wife had a painful conflict, by God's grace were able to resolve it, and then tasted the "kiss and make up" experience? It's nothing less than a taste of heaven.

But there's more. The gift of peace is never given in isolation. There are eight other attributes that form the cluster that makes life worth living. God's Holy Spirit is all set and ready to dole out these nine fruit-flavors of goodness to married couples like you who approach him in faith-filled prayer. He wants you to ask for these vital gifts. Just visualize in your mind what it feels like to be in the presence of an individual who bears the Spirit's fruit of peace, along with the other healthy fruits of the Spirit. Not just one, but *two* peace-filled people can make a very good marriage.

Read out loud the list of love, joy, and *peace* and the other characteristics, which build faithful people and strong marriages:

love	patience	faithfulness
joy	kindness	gentleness
peace	goodness	self-control

Let's apply: Which of these nine attractive characteristics caught your eye when you two first met? With grateful thanks, acknowledge God who loves you and gives you to each other.

Let's pray together: O Holy Spirit, we thank you for generously enabling us to grow spiritual fruit that maintains our family peace. Thanks for your positive influence, keeping us together, and enabling us to solve our problems with your help. Amen.

CHAPTER 12

QUALITIES THAT CONTINUE TO ATTRACT

What I want is for you to receive a well-earned reward because of your kindness.

—Philippians 4:17

Have you seen this kind of a plot in a TV drama? Scene: A 10-year high school class reunion. Characters: A girl and guy who dated each other seriously as teenagers and now reconnect for the first time after not seeing each other. Plot development: During the reunion weekend the two spend some one-to-one time together when they make a brief trip to visit and help out a classmate (who still lives in town) who cannot attend because of illness. The two of them wonder if the spark between them is still there: Are they still attracted to each other?

Flashback to the intervening years: The girl and her family move to a different city. The guy enlists in the army. After three years in the service, he gets married. Four years later they are divorced, and he has been single for two years. The girl also gets married, but her husband dies in a car accident nine years later; she has been single for a year. The story's intensity builds during the two days of the reunion, as their classmates (and TV viewers) vicariously enjoy watching them, wondering how things will turn out.

The brief trip to visit their sick classmate occurs on Sunday morning, the last day of the reunion. Their purpose: to share news of their class members gleaned during the reunion, so their sick friend won't feel left out of everything. Driving to and back from the home of their friend, they talk a great deal. They are happy to have been able to accomplish their brief mission of mercy together. But is there more?

Final scene: the reunion attendees are saying their good-byes after Sunday brunch, the closing event. The girl and guy are finishing their coffee at a corner table in the reunion restaurant. It's hard to say good-bye. First one, then the other, realizes the truth: Though it was good to see each other again, they no longer perceive each other as they did 10 years before. They hug one last time.

Let's apply: The two people in the story do *not* get back together. You and your husband or wife *are* together. Now separate yourselves from the story above. In turn, share with each other your response to the question: When you first met him/her, what were the attributes which first attracted you? Which of those attributes has grown in quality—and you appreciate now even more?

Let's pray together: Dear Lord, thank you for bringing us together in marriage. We are grateful for your help, enabling us to solve each problem as it arose. Some were resolved more quickly; others took longer. But all the while your grace deepened our love and appreciation for each other. Thank you for keeping us attracted to each other. Help us to stay faithful to each other not only outwardly, but in our innermost hearts. Keep giving us what it takes to stay very much in love. We praise you, Jesus, Amen.

CHAPTER 13

AMBIENCE FROM THE HOLY SPIRIT

Unfailing love and truth have met together. Righteousness and peace have kissed!

—Psalm 85:10

Martha Stewart often uses the word *ambience* in her TV programs, and in newspaper and magazine articles. The Oxford Concise Dictionary defines ambience as "the character and atmosphere of a place." In our day ambience is *in*. We often pair ambience with adjectives like *warm, beautiful, lovely,* or *peaceful.*

After we got married, one of our first concerns was how to furnish and decorate our home the best we could. We focused on every aspect of our house or apartment, hoping to produce effects that our visiting family and friends would find inviting and comfortable. We focused on the overall design and style of our living space, the shape, texture, and color of the walls, floors, furniture, fabrics, lighting. We understood that each contributes to our home's overall ambience.

When people first enter our house, they are met by the décor of our house. Soon after, they perceive the tone of our family relationships. In a previous devotion entitled "Qualities that Attract," I listed the Holy Spirit's attributes or "fruit" from Galatians 5:22–23: "love, joy, peace, patience, kindness, goodness, faithfulness, gentleness, and self-control."

Whether or not we as a couple bear and share those nine characteristics of the Spirit, people notice. On the one hand, if our guests sense a negative ambience, they may feel un-ease (dis-ease), and instinctively not wish to linger with us.

On the other hand, as we bear the Spirit's fruit, our guests relax and feel like taking their shoes off. They may even feel comfortable and safe enough with us to lay down a burden they've been carrying for a while. In our presence and the ambience of our home, they find some much-needed emotional rest.

That's how Henri Nouwen describes the essence of true hospitality: to offer that great gift, the unspoken but real invitation: "You may rest here." If we as a couple have received the gift of God's rest and acceptance through Christ, we will be able to pass on to our guests that same nourishing gift in the Spirit. They may even receive a measure of healing for their hearts.

Let's apply: Recall times when your guests could feel your unspoken invitation, "You may rest here," and received healing for their spirits. What physical and spiritual components of your home and presence contributed to that ambience?

Let's pray together: (Read again the sentence above from Psalm 85, which says that God's gifts of "righteousness and peace have kissed.") Thank you, dear Lord, for creating the wonderful attributes of love, including your righteousness and peace. May we share those valuable gifts with all who enter our home, whose lives we touch. In you we find rest, for you are the Source of ambience in our home. In Jesus, we pray. Amen.

CHAPTER *14*

ONE HEART, ONE ACTION

Submit to one another out of reverence for Christ.
—Ephesians 5:21

When a husband and wife defer to each other in love, respect, and service, their two hearts are ready to work together toward their major goals. Neither of them is the star; they live and work in concert with each other: "Submit to one another out of reverence for Christ" (Ephesians 5:21). Singleness of heart and action (Jeremiah 32:39) occurs when two people:

1. **Hold the same goals.** Start by trusting God. Understand that God loves you both with such intense, deep love that he was moved to send Christ to help you. He took upon himself your full humanity. The Holy Spirit moved you to say *yes* to God in faith. Having the same goals starts with believing God's promises together.

2. **Work together toward those goals.** Discuss and pray for goals worth investing your time, effort, and love. Determine the ways you'll each work toward your goals. You may not always agree on the details of exactly how you'll do each task. Pool your

individual creativities. Each contributes your unique skills, ideas, and energies toward attaining your goals.

3. **Enjoy the reward of reaching your goals.** As you reach one of your goals, celebrate. Do this by giving each other an appropriate gift, such as a card, adding beautiful words you yourself have written, a dinner out, an overnight at a B & B, a piece of furniture, an item of clothing, or a tool or toy to help you enjoy your favorite recreation (golf club, tennis racket, snowmobile gloves). You can also celebrate in ways just as meaningful while spending little or nothing. You can substitute creativity for cost.

Let's apply: Discuss and agree on the two or three main goals for your life. Write them down. Compare and consolidate your goals into one list.

Let's pray together: Dear Lord God, help us to agree on our most important life goals as a couple and a family. Help us to focus on pleasing you individually and together. Amen.

CHAPTER 15

VIVA LA DIFFERENCE!

Now there are different kinds of spiritual gifts, but it is the same Holy Spirit who is the source of them all. There are different kinds of service in the church, but it is the same Lord we are serving. There are different ways God works in our lives, but it is the same God who does the work in all of us.

—1 Corinthians 12:4–6

A man was expressing his opinion to a small group of us about the differences between men and women. He said: "The only difference is in our 'plumbing.'" We begged to differ. God had special purposes in creating us as he did. "When God created people, he made them in the likeness of God. He created them male and female, and he blessed them and called them 'human'" (Genesis 5:1b–2).

Light enters a prism as "white." When light shines out of the prism, it separates into rainbow-colored bands. Looking to God and his creative genius, we males and females can each contribute our unique gifts, blending them for the common good of God's family, the Church, and the two of us in marriage. As I quoted Paul in the passage above, "It is the same Holy Spirit who is the source of all (our gifts) . . . . There are different ways God works in our lives, but it is the same God who does the work in all of us."

In order to live in harmony with each other in the family, we depend on the Holy Spirit. He helps our egos remain under God's loving control. Paul explained it this way: "Be honest in your estimate of yourselves, measuring your value by how much faith God has given you" (Romans 12:3b).

Celebrate each other's uniqueness, rather than try to remake your partner in your image. In one kind of situation, you as the wife will make the major contribution to the common good. In another, you as the husband will provide the more dramatic help for the family's benefit. No matter.

A family psychologist made the observation that members of well-functioning families realize that there is plenty of honor to go around. Members of not-so-well-functioning families have the impression that if one person is commended, the family supply of glory will be diminished, and so they become envious. The truth is the opposite: When one family member is honored, everyone's life is enhanced.

Let's apply: Imagine running into an old friend who hasn't met your spouse and asks what he or she is like. Afterward, tell him or her what words you used. Better yet, write it in a note that your spouse can keep.

Let's pray together: Dear Lord, thank you for giving us to each other. By your Holy Spirit, protect us from a competitive spirit toward each other. Instead of our trying to outshine each other, enable us to blend our gifts for our well-being as a couple and a family. Show us how to reflect your love for all of us. In the name of Jesus. Amen.

CHAPTER 16

INTEGRITY IN ACTION

I know, my God, that you examine our hearts and rejoice when you find integrity there. You know I have done all this with good motives, and I have watched your people offer their gifts willingly and joyously.

—1 Chronicles 29:17

Self-help books often refer to the benefits of being "centered." A woman and a man who are both centered—that is, have integrity—tend to have a good marriage. Integrity is the sum of all that we are, as God has created and keeps re-creating us in Christ.

The Oxford Concise Dictionary defines integrity as the "quality of being complete; an unbroken condition, wholeness, soundness." When you see a person show that kind of wholeness in his or her actions, you feel safe. You trust her or him. In married life we observe each other functioning in all kinds of circumstances. Our trust level builds as we see each other cope in various situations without: 1) blowing up in anger, 2) becoming unduly depressed, or 3) sacrificing our morals.

Married couples and families not only impact each other's lives, they also affect the community around them. Couples who have integrity are aware not only of their own needs, but they also look outwards toward others—people in their church, workplace, and community. "Each of you should look not only to your own interests, but also to the interests of others" (Philippians 2:4, NIV).

Faith connects good intentions with effective actions. When our hearts are stirred by faith, actions that match God's will tend to follow. When others see us as a couple display unity of intention and action, they get an impression of harmony, and they are encouraged. Such harmony reflects God's love in Christ in a winsome way.

Let's apply: Discuss a couple you know, whose actions show integrity. Each of you, mention one example of their high level of integrity.

Let's pray together: Father, help our intentions flow smoothly into actions that parallel your gracious will, benefiting people. In Christ, our Lord. Amen.

CHAPTER 17

A HERITAGE
FROM THE LORD

Children are a gift from the Lord; they are a reward from him.
—Psalm 127:3

Fathers, don't aggravate your children. If you do, they will become discouraged and quit trying.

—Colossians 3:21

[I wrote this book of devotions for married couples. Some of you have children, while others do not. I wrote this devotion and the next for you who have children.]

Couples with children find that some aspects of their relationship with each other are reflected in their children. Someone has said that the best gift you can give your children is to love their mother or father. Loving each other well—not with a possessive, selfish love—is the best soil in which to raise your children. And conversely, loving your children well stimulates your marital love for each other.

But it really starts with thanking God for loving us, for giving us each other in marriage, and for giving us each of our children. Being thankful to God for our children will affect the way that we treat them—every day.

Our children thrive when we give them as much love as possible. They need a huge amount of love from us if they are to grow, flourish, and realize their potential under God.

Samuel, who grew to be a famous prophet and judge, was definitely a wanted child. His mother Hannah was unable to conceive for some years. She repeatedly prayed to God for a child. When she became pregnant, her heart bubbled with joy. When her son was born, she named him Samuel "because I asked the Lord for him" (1 Samuel 1:20).

And yet Hannah did not hold onto her beloved little son in a possessive way. Instead, after careful prayer, she decided, "I will take him and present him before the Lord, and he will live there always" (1 Samuel 1:22). It turned out that God blessed Samuel under the training of Eli, the high priest. Samuel grew to become a great and faithful servant of the Lord. God gave Samuel the awesome responsibility to serve as a judge and a prophet for the people of God.

Assuring our children that they are God's valuable gifts to us does wonders for their self-esteem. And our act of telling them how much we thank God for them has the added effect of clarifying our vision of our family. We grow in seeing our family as a total gift from God, with each child precious (though different from his or her siblings), loved by God and by us his parents.

Here is an added benefit of remembering that our children are God's gifts of love to us: it helps us avoid aggravating them. Our thankful love for them will override our being overly irritated by their missteps.

Let's apply: Research the meanings of the names of your present children, and possible names for future children. Christian bookstores have name books for babies, including possible biblical meanings. Tell your children why you were motivated to choose those names for them. Then incorporate their names and meanings in prayers offered to God in their presence.

Let's pray together: Dear Father, you are fully aware of our humanness and sinfulness. Forgive us for underestimating the value of the children you've given us. May our hearts glow with appreciation to you for these inestimable gifts to us. Create in each member of our family a steady and consistent trust in you, our God, with gratitude for your Word and promises. For Jesus' sake. Amen.

CHAPTER 18

"YOU HAVE WONDERFUL CHILDREN"

How happy are those who fear the Lord—all who follow his ways! You will enjoy the fruit of your labor. How happy you will be! How rich your life! Your wife will be like a fruitful vine, flourishing within your home. And look at all those children! There they sit around your table as vigorous and healthy as young olive trees.

—Psalm 128:1–3

Hearing someone say to you, "You have wonderful children" can make your day, your week, your month. Mark Twain said, "I can live on a good compliment for three months."

You have high expectations for your children. While those expectations are rarely all met, there are times when other adults say encouraging things about your children. When such words enter your ears, your heart receives deep comfort. Above all, hearing evidence that our children sincerely trust their Savior brings a joy unmatched in this life.

On the other hand, there will be days when we see our children fighting or failing to reach their goals in school or friendships. On those days, our hearts sink. But when we are privileged to watch their wholesome, positive behaviors and actions, that's the time to affirm them enthusiastically.

We receive personal joy and satisfaction from being part of our family. At the same time, we are aware that strong, godly families are

53

the infrastructure of our community, country, and world. As we think of our children—even when they are small—we may notice some skills and tendencies that please us greatly: "She sure reminds me of you, with her musical skill." "He is already showing dexterity in his hands, just like you." At the same time that we celebrate our children's personalities and talents, let's remember to give God the credit and thanks.

Let's pray, look for, and be prepared to commend our children for:

1. Healthy intentions and good follow-through.
2. Their ability to play alone as well as with other children and adults.
3. Their understanding that God is the giver of their skills and strengths, which are to be used for the well-being of others and for giving glory to God. Such encouragement from you lifts their hearts and strengthens their healthy behaviors.

Let's apply: When you consider your children's skills and accomplishments, how can you tell the *difference* between unwholesome self-absorption, vs. healthy self-esteem, matched by the ability to interact and enjoy being with others?

Let's pray together: Dear Lord God, we now pray for each of our children:

In regard to____, we thank you for____, and ask that you____.

In regard to____, we thank you for____, and ask that you____.

In regard to____, we thank you for____, and ask that you____.

If you have additional children, add them:

CHAPTER *19*

COMPETING OR COMPLIMENTING?

You need to know, friends, that thanking God over and over for you is not only a pleasure; it's a must . . . . Your faith is growing phenomenally; your love for each other is developing wonderfully. Why, it's only right to give thanks. We're so proud of you.

—2 Thessalonians 1:3–4 (THB)

C.S. Lewis wrote, "We delight to praise what we enjoy because the praise not merely expresses but *completes the enjoyment* . . . . The delight is incomplete till it is expressed." (Italics added.) Complimenting and praising each other is a characteristic of a healthy married relationship.

As partners, we interact with each other many times a day. When one of us takes on a project, the other acts as a sounding board, recognizing sincere intention and effective action. If we don't compliment our spouse, "The delight is incomplete till it is expressed."

Joe Murray said, "Marriage should be a duet: When one sings, the other claps." Is it shyness or self-centeredness that prevents us from complimenting each other more often? Or is it that little green-eyed imp of jealousy lurking somewhere in the corner of our heart, inciting us to competitiveness and rivalry?

In marriage, we need to replace feelings of adolescent competitiveness with new, God-grown maturity. Instead of competing, we have the unique opportunity to *complement,* that is, supplement each other's gifts and strengths. Then we'll likely *compliment* our partner, acknowledging both his or her efforts and the results of those efforts. We borrow God's eyes to see him or her. We compliment her or him for faithfully using the gifts God has granted.

Complimenting another person heals the other person's anxieties with love. Love sends fear running: "Such love has no fear because perfect love expels all fear" (1 John 4:18).

Let's apply: After reading this devotion together, give your spouse a compliment. Again tomorrow say a simple word of affirmation on the phone, or write a note to him/her. Among the things to compliment him or her for, don't forget to acknowledge his or her good judgment. You may notice how your compliment gave her or him some needed emotional rest.

Let's pray together: Lord Jesus, by your Holy Spirit, help me to be quicker to notice my spouse, and how I may fulfill his/her needs. Free me from being overly engrossed in filling my own needs. Amen.

CHAPTER 20

HOW TO GET OVER
A SPAT . . . QUICKLY

My Father the gardener, prunes the branches that do bear fruit so they will produce even more. You have already been pruned for greater fruitfulness by the message I have given you.

—John 15:2b–3

Petals on flowers are fragile, easily bruised. So are our egos. One day when my wife Julie's mother was visiting from Chicago, we were sitting out on our deck. Julie said something that mildly zinged me; I had not repaired an electrical wall plug there. Because her mom—whom we love—was there, I was more sensitive than usual.

That night as we were preparing for bed, I expressed my hurt. Julie's reply healed my feelings immediately. She said, "Deane, when I said that, I wasn't referring to your character." She separated my action from myself as a person. Putting my small misdeed into God's perspective, her words resolved the matter on the spot.

When you see a petal that has wilted on a flower, you pluck the petal rather than uproot the plant. Similarly, God cares more about us as persons than he does about our sins. He assures us that what Jesus did in redeeming us was motivated purely out of love for us. Even when God corrects us, his only motive is to heal us, and to increase our faithfulness as his children. How do you spell relief? God spells it: "I love you both. I love your marriage. I'm here to heal you now."

Let's apply: Is there some baggage from the recent past that you can deal with now, placing it in God's perspective? Do it, and taste the healing.

Let's pray together: Dear Lord our God, what can I say? Thank you for pouring your love into our lives in many detailed events, as well as in times of major transition. You come to our aid to resolve our problems. We praise your love and compassion toward us, the way you reassure us with your forgiveness. You declare us justified in your sight, all because of what Jesus did for us on the cross, and by his rising to life again. Thank you for rebuilding our lives daily. In him we pray. Amen.

CHAPTER 21

UNITED IN LOVE,

UNITED IN CHRIST

The fruit of righteousness will be peace; the effect of righteous will
be quietness and confidence forever.

—Isaiah 32:17 (NIV)

F aint heart ne'er won fair lady," wrote Cervantes, the author of *Don
Quixote*. Confidence moves you to action. Confidence keeps your
momentum going. If both persons in a marriage have a steady
sense of confidence, their love for each other will have a dynamic, interesting quality.

Rather than a macho, bravado confidence, yours will be quiet and
deep, marked by consistency and continuity. That's because your confidence is not a solo act. It is rooted in unity. You are united because you
both trust God, and are linked to your spouse by unselfish, confident
love.

The woman and man who stay in love know who they are: two individuals who've been ransomed from sin and death by the Lord Jesus.
They know that Jesus atoned for each of their sins on the cross. They
know Christ gives them God's righteousness and love as gifts, gifts God
freely extends to them, gifts that can be received only by faith.

Did you light a white unity candle at your wedding? If so, what
kinds of thoughts went through your minds as your taper touched the

wick of the large candle? In that flame did you see, not only your ardor for each other, but also a reflection of Christ's love illuminating your mutual love?

Now, after the wedding, do you still see Jesus and his light burning brightly at the center of your love and respect for each other? He is the one who keeps you united. Certain of his grace and love for you, you can grow in being confident in your relationship with each other.

Let's apply: Check your perceptions: What signals tell you your partner's confidence is up? Down?

Let's pray together: Gracious Lord Jesus, you have done it all for us. You're the source of our assets and strengths. Keep us united in love. Please build our oneness in you and in each other. Amen.

CHAPTER 22

A FULLER
UNDERSTANDING

A (person) of understanding delights in wisdom.

— Proverbs 10:23

A (person's) wisdom gives him patience.

—Proverbs 19:11

A *fuller* understanding? When we as a couple are trying to solve a problem, we may become frustrated, trying to assess the relative importance and urgency of the problem.

Knowing the importance and urgency of an issue will help us assign the appropriate time and energy to solve it. Here's one way of mentally organizing issues or challenges that helps us avoid confusion:

A $200 problem is **major** ...... serious illness, critical financial situation

A $20 problem is **medium** ...... takes good thought, can usually be solved in days

A 20 cent problem is **trivial** ...... people's lives aren't affected, no matter the outcome

Most of us tend to expend too much time and emotion in solving $20 and 20 cent problems. Then when major situations arises—say, a

$200 problem such as serious illness—we may run out of our supply of emotional energy to see it through. We've already blown our resources on the medium and "small stuff." This is a partial rather than a fuller understanding of the issues. Understanding the relative importance of problems helps us spend our energies wisely, according to the importance, not just the apparent urgency, of each matter as it arises.

Each time Julie and I were getting ready to leave Chicago to return to our home in Japan, packing seemed to loom like a major obstacle. We could feel our stress level rising. One day my father-in-law saw me struggling and simply offered, "What do you need?" He came to my aid, and before long we heard the welcome music of suitcases snapping shut. He helped us to assign the proper level of importance to packing for the overseas trip. It was a $20 problem.

Let's apply: In the three categories, insert three examples of issues, assigning to each its appropriate level of importance:

Major ($200): _____

Medium: ($20) _____

Minor: (20 cent) _____

Let's pray together: Lord Jesus, please provide us with your wisdom to understand the relative "size" of each issue we're working on. Help us grow toward a fuller understanding of our various challenges, so that we can not only accomplish tasks but treat each other fairly, with respect and love. Amen.

CHAPTER 23

A PROFOUND MYSTERY

"A man leaves his father and mother and is joined to his wife and the two are united into one." This is a great mystery, but it is an illustration of the way Christ and the church are one.

—Ephesians 5:31–32

Mysteries are interesting. Movies and TV shows are full of them. A story situation is portrayed as so difficult, we don't see how it can be solved. Watching fictional stories from the safety of our family room, we are transported from our present reality. It's entertaining to watch the mystery unfold on the screen.

As married people, we also encounter mysteries. We may not fully understand our spouse. We ask ourselves: "Why does he or she feel that way? How did this problem develop? How can we get through it safely?"

Try this: In your own mind, imagine that you and your husband/wife are interacting as if you were characters in a drama. Mentally stepping outside your actual situation for a brief time can provide you a feeling of safe detachment and freedom so you can think creatively. Temporarily stepping outside yourselves enables you to "think outside the box."

One thing more: We may feel overwhelmed by a situation; it may seem too huge to tackle. Instead of trying to solve the entire problem, choose one part of it. Warm up by addressing one smaller, easy-to-handle portion of the issue. Before long, you may find you're over the hump and relaxed enough to address one of the larger parts of the problem. Using this method will help increase your confidence in yourself and your ability to conquer problems.

Let's apply: Recall an interesting story that you have read. Remember your anticipation as you moved toward the resolution of the mystery? Knowing that the facts will ultimately come to light relaxes you. You are freed to enjoy the process as it unfolds. This method of placing your situation into an imaginary, hypothetical setting can help you think logically and objectively.

Let's pray together: Help us, dear Lord, not to be "spooked" by the mysteries we encounter in our life together. Give us anticipatory joy as we wait for these mysteries to unfold. Remember these words of God? "For I know the plans I have for you, declares the Lord, plans to prosper you and not to harm you, plans to give you hope and a future" (Jeremiah 29:11, NIV). "Though you have not seen him, you love him; and even though you do not see him now, you believe in him and are filled with an inexpressible and glorious joy" (1 Peter 1:8, NIV). Amen.

CHAPTER 24

TWO MOUTHS, ONE WORD OF PRAISE

Glorify the Lord with me; let us exalt his name together.

—Psalm 34:3

Gene* and Fran (short for Francesca)* were spending an enjoyable day off together, a month or so before their wedding. On Tuesday of that week, they found out unexpectedly that both of them wouldn't have to go in to work on Thursday. It was like getting a freebie gift. Gene said, "That'll give us time to go to the photographer's, and maybe work out some things with the reception hall."

"That'll be great," agreed Fran. "You know, honey, that won't take but an hour or so—since they're both less than a mile from each other. . . . I bet we could do both of them and still have the rest of the day to do something fun. What would you like to do?"

"We could put our bikes on the car rack. And since both the photographer's and the reception hall are on the south side of town, in Apple Valley, after we're done with them, we can just keep on going south, to Cannon Falls, and go riding on the Cannon Valley Trail. What do *you* think?"

So on the Wednesday they phoned the photographer and the reception hall office, to say they'd like to stop by between 9:00 and 10:00 the

* Not real names.

next morning. On Thursday, they accomplished their two errands, and they were on their way. They arrived at the trailhead by 11:00 a.m. They stopped at 1:00 for delicious corned beef sandwiches at the Family Deli in Red Wing, and cycled back to Cannon Falls in the afternoon. On their way back, they stopped at Applebee's for an early supper. "Today was a real serendipity," Fran said, as Gene dropped her and her bike off at her place. "Yeah, a true, unexpected pleasure," responded Gene. "And having a spontaneous fun day like this helped me relax. I feel less uptight about the rest of the things we need to get done before the wedding. Today was God's gift to us."

Fran agreed. But they realized that, greater than having the day off to relax, was the gift of learning something about each other. They found out they both had a capacity for spontaneity. It was a welcome discovery that would serve them well in their married life. Gene said, "Thanks, honey, for your idea that we could accomplish those two tasks first thing in the morning, and still be able to spend the major part of the day in recreation." They were thankful to God and grateful to each other.

What we think most highly of, we praise most enthusiastically. Our voices have a lilt to them, almost as if we're singing. We set our sights higher. We praise the values, assets, goals, and dreams of each other. *And* we praise God.

Thank God for all the love you're receiving from him. Thank him for his wonderful attributes. Praise him for his wonderful gifts. Praise him individually in your heart. And praise him together as a couple.

Praise God not only for what he does for you. Praise him also *for himself.*

Let's apply: Discuss the relationship between praising God and complimenting each other. Pray a prayer in which you praise God for himself, and then thank him for what he does for you.

Let's pray together: We praise and adore you, O Lord, for being the God you *are.* You have promised to accept all our prayers offered in the name of Jesus, including our praises. We thank you for giving us each other, allowing us to be together as a couple. In our Savior's loving name. Amen.

CHAPTER 25

POWER LISTENING

When others are happy, be happy with them. If they are sad, share their sorrow.

—Romans 12:15

At certain times, when talking with your spouse, the tone of the conversation may turn serious; and you may feel trapped. Continuing to listen can be hard work, but if you can each listen to each other well, your relationship will likely continue to grow.

The best preparation for listening to others is to prayerfully practice hearing God's voice. Eli taught young Samuel to respond when God would call him by saying: "Yes, Lord, your servant is listening" (1 Samuel 3:9).

When we practice hearing God's voice, the Holy Spirit leads us out of fear and confusion and into calm, clear listening. Power listening to God dissolves our fears and tunes our ears so we can patiently take in and ponder what our spouse is saying.

Our resistance to listening to each other settles down to a manageable level. We feel much less intimidated and on the defensive. Practicing power listening is well worth it. When we listen with a patient, non-judgmental attitude, the one who is speaking will feel peacefully invited to say what's on his or her heart. We become confident that we'll be able to handle what we hear, and then respond appropriately, free of anger or fear.

Roll God's name around in your heart and on your tongue. Hearing and speaking God's name builds trust and peace within your spirit. With God's assurance that he won't desert you, you are ready to listen to each other. Listening with love enables you to "Be happy when others are happy. And if they are sad, share their sorrow" (Romans 12:15).

Let's apply: With an attitude of honesty and transparency, ask each other in turn: "Do you feel that I hear you and understand what you are saying?"

Let's pray together: Thank you, dear Lord, for reassuring us that you love us. Thank you for calming our fears. Teach us to listen to you attentively and to each other effectively. In the name of our Redeemer. Amen.

CHAPTER 26

A WHOLESOME

LOVE TRIANGLE

A friend loves at all times . . . .

—Proverbs 17:17

. . . There is a friend who sticks closer than a brother.

—Proverbs 18:24b

A favorite expression often included in wedding programs is, "I am marrying my best friend." The phrase points to a hoped-for bond of love, understanding, and trust between a wife and husband. In the wedding service you both promised before God, "I pledge you my faithfulness." You vowed not to become involved with any other man or woman.

Normally, a love triangle causes conflict in a marriage—not a good thing. But there is a special kind of love triangle that is held together by wholesome love between God, you, and your spouse: "A cord of three strands is not quickly broken," wrote Solomon in Ecclesiastes (4:12). A woman and a man joined with God in *this* spiritual triangle are not weakened but made strong. They are able to carry a much greater load of healthy responsibility because God is the "senior partner" of the relationship.

This triangle is marked by peace and mutual upbuilding. It provides security and protection. Couples who depend on God for their daily strength are significantly stronger than couples who try to rely on their own human resources alone.

God wants our marriages to work out successfully. He has all the resources in the universe to help us cope with the situations we encounter. Jesus said, "Surely I am with you always, to the very end of the age" (Matthew 28:20). He stays with us in our marriages and families. Jesus sacrificed himself to reconcile us to God and to each other. For this reason, God forgives us and accepts us. He renews our marriages daily, making us into new people in Christ over and over again. He enables us to live at peace with each other.

Even in their golden years these couples experience new growth, like trees producing green leaves in springtime: "They will still bear fruit in old age, they will stay fresh and green . . ." (Psalm 92:14b, NIV).

Let's apply: Think of two couples who live different lifestyles from each other: One couple depends on themselves, thinking they have only themselves and their own resources to protect and maintain their marriage. The other depends on God for renewing their love and their marriage. At the same time, they serve as conduits for others, passing on God's living water to them.

Use your imagination and think graphically: If you were to choose a particular color to describe each of the two marriages, which colors would you choose? What color is *your* marriage?

Let's pray together: Thank you for this loving triangular relationship we have with you and each other. Weave us together in love. Color our relationship with your unique peace, which transcends all human attempts at happiness. In Jesus our peace-producer. Amen.

CHAPTER 27

TWO ARE BETTER

DEFENDED-I

If one person falls, the other can reach out and help. But people who are alone when they fall are in real trouble.

—Ecclesiastes 4:10

W hat would happen if one of you were to become ill? In marriage, God created a mutual support system that is duplicated in no other relationship.

Imagine this scenario: Your wife or husband gets sick and has to take a disability leave. You are strongly motivated to help. You think creatively how to meet his or her needs and the needs of your family. You adjust. Your family stays above water financially. You're not victims, you're successful survivors.

You are surprised at the mental and emotional focus you were able to maintain—more than you thought possible. You find you're able to extend yourself with extra energy and composure. You get over each successive hump and endure until things return to normal. You are strengthened when your partner acknowledges your efforts: "Thanks for all you've done to hold things together, and for hanging in there for us. Thanks for continuing to encourage me."

There were days you got tired. A few times you even wondered how long you could keep up the pace. But you kept your emotional balance.

You worked hard because you knew what you were doing mattered. Slowly your hope returned. You knew God's promises were meant for you. Your sense of satisfaction was muted but sweet.

Let's apply: It's one thing to see a couple facing a challenge (like being laid off from work) by looking to God for strength and working together to please him. It's another to see them depending only on themselves for strength to survive. Identify some of the differences.

Let's pray: Gracious God, we thank you for supporting us with your strength and endurance. We couldn't make it without you. Lord Jesus, thank you for never giving up on us. Amen.

CHAPTER 28

TWO ARE BETTER
DEFENDED-II

If two lie down together, they will keep warm. But how can one keep warm alone?

—Ecclesiastes 4:10

An important principle in physics is that for every force there is an equal and opposite counter-force. While marriage is a powerful and important force for good in this world, there are forces that oppose and challenge our well-being in marriage. The devil, though not equal to God, would like to undermine our happiness and the health of our marriage.

Satan tries to capitalize on accidents, losses of jobs, or illnesses. He tempts us to become mean-spirited, bitter, or despondent; to become involved with another woman or man; to become frustrated over money; to forget that God is the source of everything we have and need. There are times in almost every marriage when the ill winds of adversity blow cold and rattle our rafters.

Nevertheless, God gives us tools to make our marriage work. He gives us grace to relate to each other at very deep levels, enabling us to discuss virtually everything with each other. Talking often allays anxiety and serves as a healthy reality check, protecting us from deceiving ourselves.

"If one falls down, his friend (husband or wife) can help him up." We can monitor each other's well-being. We're aware when our spouse is becoming overextended, stressed, or vulnerable. We can help each other turn away from temptation, holding onto our all-important motivation and joy.

We remind each other that God helps us not only *around,* but also *through* our challenges. He stretches us at such times. Otherwise, why would we keep on anticipating the joys of heaven when God's complete joy will be ours? Like Robert Browning wrote in his poem: "Ah, but a man's reach should exceed his grasp, or what's a heaven for?"

Let's apply: Take turns reviewing a time when your spouse helped you avoid a medium or major mistake. You and he or she had an adequate defense system, provided by God. Express your thanks.

Let's pray together: Our Father, help us to be there for each other, especially when one of us is vulnerable. We thank you for our healthy defense system—your love well at work in our marriage. In our Savior's power we pray. Amen.

CHAPTER 29

OUR MORNING LIGHT

Weeping may go on all night, but joy comes with the morning.
—Psalm 30:5

A re you a *morning* person or a *night* person? How about your spouse? If the two of you are different in this way, how do you accommodate yourselves to each other?

If you are a morning person, you will be happy to read this news: On a morning radio show on Station WCCO in Minneapolis/St. Paul, Minnesota, research results were quoted to the effect that, on average, we are twice as productive in the a.m. as in the p.m. However, that report didn't mention the fact that the night person's "morning" starts later and may well extend into the p.m.

Whichever of the two you happen to be, the Bible mentions activities appropriate for both evenings and mornings. As you are going to bed tonight, think of the verse in Ephesians (4:26), "Do not let the sun go down while you are still angry." Or check out this before-you-shut-your-eyes prayer from Psalm 4:8, "I will lie down and sleep in peace, for you alone, O Lord, make me dwell in safety" (NIV). As final thoughts about the day with your spouse cross your mind, accept God's forgiveness for yourself, and share words of forgiveness with each other—words that come to you from the heart of the God of love.

Then when you get up in the morning, no matter what happened the day before, greet the new day God has given you two in holy marriage. How about singing God's praises while taking your morning shower? "It is good to praise the Lord and make music to your name, O Most High, to *proclaim your unfailing love in the morning,* your faithfulness in the evening" (Psalm 92:1–2, NIV). Praising God pumps the adrenalin of your faith: "As for me, I will sing about your power. I will *shout with joy each morning* because of your unfailing love" (Psalm 59:16).

It's interesting that the psalm writer mentions *shouting,* not just *singing.* I think he wanted us to open our hearts—singing *or* shouting—to focus on God and enthusiastically thank him who is the "giver of every good and perfect gift" (James 1:17). There is no need to feel self-conscious about the quality of our singing voices.

Let's apply: Take a few minutes and pray a simple morning prayer in behalf of each other, one at a time.

Let's pray together: Thank you for Jeremiah's words: "The unfailing love of the Lord never ends! By his mercies we have been kept from complete destruction. Great is his faithfulness; his mercies begin afresh each day" (Lamentations 3:22–23). We pray, confident of Jesus' compassion for us. Amen.

CHAPTER 30

TRIPLE YOUR STRENGTH

As we talk to our God and Father about you, we think of your faithful work, your loving deeds, and your continual anticipation of the return of our Lord Jesus Christ.

—1 Thessalonians 1:3

One of the principles of Stephen Covey's *Seven Habits of Highly Successful People* is that of *synergy*. Covey maintains that when two people work well together, they reinforce each other's strength and efforts, so much so that they produce not just double the results of one person, but three or four times as much.

When a woman and a man function well in their marriage, welcoming God into their relationship, they become like a strong "cord of three strands" (a triple-braided cord). They no longer depend only on each other, but they trust God and receive strength from him. They look to him as their Creator and Redeemer. They ask the Holy Spirit to guide them. The quality of their married life improves, with positive joy spilling over into their work life as well.

There will be times when we as a couple "hit the wall" of painful experiences and setbacks. Here also the three-strands or synergy principle applies. At such times we need God and each other the most! We receive from God and our spouse the very support we need—support that is freely provided without condescension or judgment.

Each time we meet such a challenge in our family life, we realize that even while our relationship is being tested, God is also strengthening, nourishing, and firming us in faith and love. We can thank God and affirm each other's "faithful work, loving deeds, and endurance inspired by hope in our Lord Jesus Christ." (1 Thessalonians 1:3, NIV).

Let's apply: Reflect on one or two stormy times you've already been through together. What did you learn about God, yourself, and each other? Following those experiences, did you find yourself more apt to receive help from each other, without either of you becoming co-dependent? Or did the pain you were experiencing at the time drive a wedge between you two?

Let's pray together: Help us as a couple, Lord, to maximize our strengths as we work in full concert with each other, under you. Amen.

CHAPTER 31

THAT'S THE GLORY

OF LOVE

God is love. And all who live in love live in God, and God lives in them. And as we live in God, our love grows more perfect. So we will not be afraid on the day of judgment, but we can face him with confidence because we are like Christ here in this world. Such love has no fear because perfect love expels all fear.

—1 John 4:16b–18a

The refrain of a popular song a few years ago went: "That's the story of, that's the glory of love." Love is glorious because it expresses acceptance of the person loved. Being accepted by another provides us powerful security and fulfillment, a glorious feeling. We value the gift of love so highly because we not only receive the embrace of being accepted, but obstacles such as fear shrink and can disappear.

The Bible passage above does not use the word glory, but it's there between the lines. Living in love, that is, living in relationship with God, is glorious. Although we won't experience the full glory of being in his presence until we enter heaven, we can have real foretastes of it now in our marriage.

The passage above speaks of God's perfect love. When we are in full thrall and thrill of romantic love, we may use the word *perfect* to describe our loved one, though we know there is some exaggeration. God's love, on the other hand, *is perfect,* because God is perfect. He is full of light. There's no darkness in him at all. Being accepted by God now gives us confidence that God will accept us on judgment day. That sense of security frees us to love our wife or husband. And our love for each other continues to grow in quality and depth.

John explains that "fear has to do with punishment," while God's "perfect love expels all fear." Jesus himself absorbed the punishment we deserved due to our sins. God freed us from the oppression of our sins, assured us of his love, and equipped us with the ability to love.

Let's apply: Since the beginning of creation, people have had a strong sense that esthetic beauty helps express the glory of love. What is the most beautiful gift you've ever received from your spouse? What piece of jewelry, music CD or tape, new item of clothes or other gift has given you special joy? Though we are grateful for these gifts, we're aware they are only a down payment of the full glory of God we'll experience when we meet our Savior in heaven.

Let's pray together: Lord God, remind us of the wonders of your grace. Shine on us with the glow of your Son's glorious resurrection. Amen.

CHAPTER 32

VOWS WELL KEPT
AND MAINTAINED

Marriage should be honored by all, and the marriage bed kept pure.
—Hebrews 13:4 (NIV)

God designed the relationship of marriage to be highly respected. Our society, as reflected in TV, movies, and the commercialization of sex, has seriously eroded this respect. We've allowed dark shadows to fall on God's gift of marital fidelity.

Most people are aware of the great benefits of faithfulness in marriage. And yet for many, infidelity is not considered a major problem. The big question for you and me is: How can we escape the temptations of adultery and unfaithfulness? And other questions follow: How can we keep our lines of communication open? How can we stay in love for the rest of our lives? Jesus answers, "With man this is impossible, but with God all things are possible" (Matthew 19:26, NIV).

This book has emphasized several themes:

First, marriage is God's great gift, and we are God's gifts to each other.
Second, acknowledging God as the one who sent Jesus to atone for our sins gives us confidence that God loves and protects both us and our marriage.

Third, slowing the pace of our lifestyle even a little helps us savor God's gifts and allows us opportunity to get to know and understand each other more deeply.

Fourth, God doesn't force His spiritual and material blessings on us. God gently guides us, promising, "Your ears will hear a voice behind you saying, 'This is the way; turn around and walk here'" (Isaiah 30:21, NIV).

Fifth, filling our voids—whether in one of us or in our relationship—will both prevent conflict and enhance our mutual joy in Christ.

Sixth, let's associate with the most positive, faithful couples with whom we are comfortable. They will also help us stay accountable.

Welcome the lift God's Holy Spirit provides you in these devotions to settle your heart, redirect your emotions, and give you hope. Trust God to enable you to do what you cannot do by yourselves: stay in love for a lifetime.

Let's apply: The devotions in this book are building blocks to help you love each other for the rest of your life. What are specific things you can do to help yourself and your spouse avoid temptations to unfaithfulness?

Let's pray together: Dear Lord God, help us not merely to tolerate a maintenance type of marriage that settles for minimum joy. Help us be content, but at the same time keep our growing edge. Strengthen us to stay pure and faithful to you and each other, as we promised in our marriage vows. In Jesus. Amen.

CHAPTER 33

A GREAT SENSE

OF TIMING

When we were utterly helpless, Christ came at just the right time and
died for us sinners.

—Romans 5:6

Our tulips, crocuses, and daffodils bloomed at the very time we
were beginning to wonder if spring would *ever* come. They
have a built-in biological clock. Timing is vital—though not
necessarily built in—if you are a mother, a father, an actor, an athlete,
a surgeon, or a person who runs a high-tech machine. Good timing
is crucial when you are driving on the freeway, cooking hamburgers
on a grill, proposing marriage, closing a sale, or interviewing for a job
position.

A wise person categorized people into two types: those who function
like *accountants,* and those who function like *race car drivers.* Accountants work methodically, usually exhibiting an even emotional state,
while race car drivers need to make quick decisions in the excitable
atmosphere of a race. Neither type is better. Neither should command
more respect than the other. Nonetheless, in both, a well-honed sense
of timing is very beneficial.

My wife has more of the accountant skills and instincts, while
I have more of the race car driver. Most often we complement and

balance each other's gifts and leanings. We also help shore up each other's weaknesses and ungifted areas.

This arrangement is very helpful in marriage: when we work together in love, we watch each other's actions, so that if a weakness in one of us begins to appear, the other can sound the alert, thus saving him or her from possible embarrassment. By our spouse bringing to our attention a potential problem that could arise from an unbridled weakness of ours, he or she helps us "nip it in the bud." A loving action, done at just the right time, is worth more than gold.

Though each of us tends toward one of the two types, we also have some of both types of person within us. There are times when we must make quick decisions, while at other times a methodical approach is more effective. God's love has the effect of either stimulating us to appropriate action or calming our nerves in a tense situation.

Let's apply: Mention a situation when you need to make a quick, responsible decision:

_____

Mention a situation when you need to make deliberate, thought-through decisions:

_____

Let's pray together: Gracious Lord, thank you for sending Jesus to our side at just the right time. Thank you for our parents and others who help us hear God's Word in a timely way. May your Holy Spirit give us a strong sense of timing: when to speed up, when to slow down, when to wait, and when to act decisively. In Jesus. Amen.

CHAPTER 34

PERFECTION OR COMPLETION?

Every time I think of you, I give thanks to my God. And I am sure that God, who began the good work within you, will continue his work until it is finally finished on the day when Christ Jesus comes back again.

—Philippians 1:3, 6

Modern mass media is glitzy, but not always truthful. Models' faces and bodies are propped, primped, and primed for the TV cameras in ways that sometimes alter reality. Viewers can build up false, unrealistic expectations about what they "should" look like.

Viewing ourselves and others according to external appearances is very incomplete and misleading. God looks at what's in our hearts and minds. He knows the full reality of who we really are.

Getting ready for your wedding, you worked carefully to make your appearance—including your clothes and cosmetics—as nearly "perfect" as you could. In the succeeding days, your spouse has seen you in your reality: when you were tired or worried, sick, just got out of bed, or just came in from mowing the lawn. He or she has come to accept you in the whole range of your appearance and emotional states.

In Paul's Word of God in Philippians quoted above, he mentions that God gladly monitors our well-being and tenderly guides our growth. Under our heavenly Father's care, we are very much a work in progress:

"God, who began the good work within you, will continue his work until it is finished on the day when Christ Jesus comes back again." Trusting God to guide us toward completion is much better than trying to fake perfection in this imperfect world.

Let's apply: Recall a time when you were not at your best and your partner accepted you anyway. Express warm thanks to him or her. Extend that same love and courtesy when she or he is not at the top of her or his game.

Let's pray together: We remember how you sacrificed yourself in love for us, Lord Jesus. We are not star-crossed lovers (as Romeo and Juliet referred to each other), but Christ-crossed lovers, forgiven and free to grow, because of what you accomplished for us on the cross. You are protecting and guiding us until the day when you return and complete our life with God. Thank you, dear Lord, for working in me and my husband/wife to accept our marriage as a work in progress. And you, O Lord, are guiding our progress. Amen.

CHAPTER 35

FOUR STEPS OF
A REAL APOLOGY

Confess your sins to each other and pray for each other so that you may be healed. The prayer of a righteous person has great power and wonderful results.

—James 5:16

So, who is a righteous person? Answer: A person is righteous when God declares that Jesus has made that person righteous by sacrificing himself for him or her.

Important Benefit No.1: God promises to hear the prayers of a person offered in the name of Jesus.

Important Benefit No.2: You now have the capacity to confess your sins, without being afraid your confession won't be accepted. You know you'll be forgiven. Use these four steps as your **Let's apply** assignment for today:

1. **Describe the situation,** the circumstances in which you messed up. Be as accurate and objective as you can in describing the setting.
2. **Describe what you did or did not do.** Don't sugarcoat or excuse yourself. Again, be objective in saying exactly what you did. Hold back from expressing regret or shame at this point. Sidestep self-pity.

3. **Describe the resulting damage** of your ill-chosen action. Who was hurt, and in what way?
4. **Then express your apology in simple words.** Say something like, "Please forgive me for _____."

You have "thrown yourself on the mercy of the court." Don't rush to fill the quietness with more words. Wait for the other person to respond.

Further action may not be necessary, though you may need to make restitution. Don't dwell on that issue *before* you apologize. An honest confession often has the welcome effect of clearing the air, so that if or when the issue of restitution is discussed, you and others involved can think clearly and bring closure to the incident.

You will never regret apologizing. Before God and in your heart, you will know that was the appropriate thing to do. A real apology works like climbing a mountain. Once you do it, then from that new vantage point, you will see your next step. Use the Four Steps outlined here. Use them one at a time, in sequence, and watch them work.

Let's pray together: Dear gracious Lord, please send us your Holy Spirit to provide that small but necessary boost of courage and energy, so we can use these Four Steps of a Real Apology. We recall the solid promise from the Psalm (51:17), "The sacrifice you want is a broken spirit. A broken and repentant heart, O God, you will not despise." Thank you. We needed that. In the name of the One who declares us righteous even *while* we're apologizing, we pray. Amen.

CHAPTER 36

"I'M TALKING MOSTLY TO MYSELF"

Is there any encouragement from belonging to Christ? . . . Then make me truly happy by agreeing wholeheartedly with each other, loving one another, and working together with one heart and purpose.
—Philippians 2:1–2

Sometimes my wife Julie and I use the helpful phrase "I'm talking mostly to myself" when evaluating something we did or said that didn't work out the way we'd hoped. For example, we've been together with some friends. Riding home in the car, we talk about the evening, and rerun what we said.

Sometimes we're still savoring the good time we had with our friends. Other times we may not feel good about what happened. One or the other of us thinks he or she didn't act appropriately. In a repentant mood one of us says, "I'm talking mostly to myself . . . I hope to handle things differently next time."

It may be that one of us didn't act well. In either case, the tendency might be to accuse each other. Even if we say, "*We* didn't say the right thing," it may still come out sounding like "*You* didn't say the right thing." Our words may have the effect of accusing the other. Therefore, by saying "I'm talking mostly to myself," we accept personal responsibility without blaming the other.

The other spouse may wish to join in expressing repentance by saying, "I didn't exactly help the situation either." At least we avoided a potential trap, a conflict that could have embroiled us in an unproductive blame game.

Let's apply: Try using the phrase "I'm talking mostly to myself" in analyzing a recent event that didn't turn out as well as you had hoped. Assess the truth of what you did or didn't do. Did using that phrase help you defuse negative feelings?

Let's pray together: Gracious Lord, thank you for each time during our married life when we avoided getting into a conflict with each other by either or both of us apologizing. By your Holy Spirit's presence and power, aid us to grow in being gracious and honest. Help us restrain our "trigger finger" from blaming and shaming each other. Keep us loving and honest, as we "work together with one heart and purpose." In Jesus' name. Amen.

Part 2

DEVOTIONS FOR THE MATURE YEARS OF MARRIAGE

INTRODUCTION

On April 11, 1951, President Harry Truman appointed General Matthew Ridgway to replace General Douglas MacArthur as Supreme Commander in the Far East for the Allied Forces during the Korean War.

General Ridgway was headquartered in Korea. Because Korea was a combat zone, General Ridgway's and other high officers' wives stayed in Japan. It was a lonely time for the Ridgways. An idea occurred to them that not only comforted them in their loneliness, but also strengthened and defended them against the pressures of wartime stress.

Each evening at their separate locations, they read the *same devotion* from the same page of the same devotional book. At a predetermined time, they talked on the phone and shared their thoughts based on what they had read. Then they took turns praying, presenting their heartfelt petitions and thanksgivings to God over the wires. This story is told on page 153 in the devotion entitled "Devotions on the Road."

I hope the devotions in this book serve as preventive spiritual medicine for you and your spouse. We couples need the stimulation God provides us in his Word and delivers through our faith. He does not buy into the stereotype that people in their "golden years" should be relatively quiescent and inactive. We need spiritual nourishment from him to maintain our energy level and his guidance to keep our outlook balanced and positive.

With the longevity for both women and men steadily increasing, many of us maintain very active lifestyles. No matter how active or inactive we may be, we all face problems that occur due to various kinds of voids or vacuums that can develop in our relationship.

It may be a temporary vacuum of loneliness due to special circumstances, as the Ridgways experienced during the Korean War. Or it may be a chronic vacuum, a kind of rut where we're in a state of low or no growth, "down a quart" in emotional and spiritual strength.

In any case, our voids need to be filled. The devotions in this book are intended to fill your voids in health-enhancing, stimulating ways. I pray that the Holy Spirit will grant you both a hearty increase of joy. One of the ways Julie and I fill our needs for joy is with music—hearing, singing, and playing it. And thankfully, it leaves no unpleasant after-taste.

It shouldn't embarrass us that we have these voids, these very real needs. The truth is that we all have a whole multitude of needs. We all need to have our personal and marital resources renewed constantly. With God's help, we hope to finish strong in our marriage till death parts us.

May you be enriched as you read the words of this book. I hope you read these words together. And may you find the **Let's apply** and **Let's pray together** activities useful.

CHAPTER 37

MATURE LOVE
AT ANY AGE

Once I was young, and now I am old. Yet I have never seen the godly forsaken, nor seen their children begging for bread. The godly give generous loans to others, and their children are a blessing.
—Psalm 37:25–26

I remember the day my father died. We received the news by cablegram in Japan where we lived. After receiving the news, I phoned my mother in Chicago.

My parents had been saving for a trip to see us in Japan. On the phone I urged Mom to consider coming by herself: "Why don't you come anyway, since you have the money saved for the plane fare?" She accepted and four months later we welcomed her at the airport. She stayed with us for a year. After she arrived, Julie and I prayed the Lord would use us to comfort and help her.

As we listened and watched the ways she expressed her grief, the most noteworthy fact was not what we saw, but what we did *not* see in her: we did not see *regret*. Though she missed my dad terribly, we did not see signs of guilt or "if only I had." She was thankful for Dad and their married life. I would characterize their married love as mature love, and her grief as a *clean grief,* not muddied by unresolved issues or "what ifs."

That gave me tremendous relief, helping to heal my own grief.

Two people can love each other with real maturity no matter how old they are. Couples can love each other with understanding, wisdom, and enthusiasm whether they are in their twenties, forties, sixties or whatever age.

In our consumer-oriented American culture, idealized images of physical youthfulness tend to be idolized. But couples who are maturing spiritually, mentally, and emotionally can set the pace for the rest of us, providing us with rich resources of wisdom, love, and courage.

It is a pleasure to spend time with an older couple who seem to be obviously in love with each other (I almost wrote *still in love* with each other . . . Should it surprise us?). They seem to accept themselves and each other with honest respect and graciousness. They appear to know themselves quite well, because God's love and acceptance of them has "sunk in." Therefore, they don't need to play games of pride, or show off in front of each other to make points.

Mature love is strong love. As couples mature, they realize the impact of God's love on themselves and the mark they're making on their family, friends, and community. Not only do the couples themselves benefit, but other people around them are inspired, enjoying the warmth of their depth and maturity. After friends have been in their presence for a little while, they seem unconsciously to relax and allow their tensions to melt away.

Let's apply: Call to mind a couple you both admire. Invite them over for coffee and dessert. Notice the words they use when speaking to each other, words carefully chosen and respectfully spoken, "like apples of gold in settings of silver" (Proverbs 25:11, NIV). If you know their children, look for signs of their parents' character qualities reappearing in them and in the grandchildren.

Let's pray together: Heavenly Father, you are the one who brought us together. You are fashioning and improving our love as we learn important lessons from older married friends. Thank you for the way they are influencing us for good. In Christ, whose love cleanses and refines our love. Amen.

CHAPTER 38

LOVE COVERS
BEAUTIFULLY

Love covers over a multitude of sins.

—1 Peter 4:8

When a Japanese woman wears a formal *kimono,* she binds it together with an *obi.* An *obi* is a sash that can vary in width, top to bottom, from three to ten inches. *Obi* are very colorful, decorative, and are often made of embroidered silk.

Obi are beautiful articles of clothing, but they hide a secret. The *obi* itself does not function as a belt to hold the *kimono* together. Traditionally, all women's *kimono*s are sewn the same length, long. Underneath the *obi,* several ties bind the folds of the *kimono* at the waist so that the length of the garment fits the woman's height, and is even on all sides. The ties in themselves are not esthetically pleasing, but without them the outfit would be a disaster.

But when the *obi* is put on over them, the ties and folds of cloth are covered, and the outfit is complete. The *obi* coordinates all parts of the *kimono* into a unified whole. The wearer is now ready to go to a formal event like a wedding or New Year's Day visits.

The wide *obi* sash adds the important, finishing touch to a Japanese woman's *kimono.* As you look at the Japanese writing for *obi* below, doesn't the middle of the character suggest a belt or sash for the waist?

The *obi* covers all those not-so-beautiful-but-functionally-necessary ties underneath it. The *obi* reminds us of Peter's words,

> Love covers over a multitude of sins.
>
> —1 Peter 4:8

And the Japanese translation of Paul's words in Colossians 3:14 actually uses the word *obi*: "And over all these virtues (compassion, kindness, humility, patience, and forgiveness), put on love which binds them all together in perfect unity, like an *obi*."

As the *obi* covers and completes a *kimono* outfit, so God's love covers our sins and missteps. God offers his love to us as a free gift, only asking that we accept it in faith and apply his forgiveness to ourselves and others. When the love we've received from Christ is blended into our relationships, hurts are healed and misunderstandings dissolve. In marriage, we have daily opportunities to apply the *obi* of God's love to cover both our own misdeeds and those of our spouse.

Let's apply: As you think of your own marriage, take note that when unity prevails, a certain restfulness, peace, and ambience can be felt in the atmosphere. Intentionally plan your activities this weekend to create a slower pace, a peaceful atmosphere that covers things that need to be covered in forgiveness and forgetfulness.

Let's pray together: Merciful Father, in our life together we often encounter differences of opinion, and sometimes conflicts. Enable us to accept your love and use it effectively to reconcile our differences and heal our emotions. Help us to grow in appreciating the beauty of your word, the promise of your love in Christ Jesus. Amen.

CHAPTER 39

STAYING FRESH
AND GREEN

Even in old age the godly will still produce fruit; they will stay vital
and green. They will declare, "The Lord is just! He is my Rock. There
is nothing but good in him."

—Psalm 92:14–15

W hen we got married, we promised to stay together "till death
parts us." Some couples set their expectation-sights too low,
so their marriage lacks the excitement that accompanies
healthy growth: "Whoever sows sparingly will also reap sparingly" (2
Corinthians 9:6a, NIV).

It's wonderful when a couple makes a good beginning in their
marriage. To sustain a marriage over the long haul takes more. Some
couples experience rough waters when they become empty nesters.
Others struggle during mid-life crises and menopause. They begin dis-
tancing themselves from God and each other and gradually withdraw
from both.

But there's good news: "Whoever sows generously will also reap generously" (1 Corinthians 9:6b, NIV), because "those who live to please the
Spirit, will harvest everlasting life from the Spirit" (Galatians 6:8b).

Expect to stay fresh and green, and continue to grow spiritually by
daily devotions and praying together. You will produce fruit not only

in your early and middle years, but also in your senior years. Aim to be productive as long as you live, pointing your efforts and energies toward the goal of sharing Christ with each other and as many other people as possible. Be open to the Holy Spirit's opening God's Word to you. As a by-product, the Spirit will also reveal God's will for your life, his "good, pleasing and perfect will" (Romans 12:2c, NIV).

In your mind's eye, picture what you expect your golden years to feel and look like. Don't settle for merely coexisting with each other. Aim for fulfilled joy, savoring the "fresh fruit" of God's many blessings for years to come.

Let's apply: Describe two couples you're acquainted with: one couple is simply coexisting, while the other "stays vital and green." How can you become like that second couple, who continue being productive for God for all of the time they have on earth?

Let's pray together: Dear righteous God, help us to accept your gift of married love as a "many-splendored thing," not settling for low-growth hopes. Give us a marriage that stays fresh and green for the rest of our time here. By faith we accept Jesus' loving sacrifice of himself, his promises, forgiveness, and righteousness, as the incomparable gifts they are. Amen.

CHAPTER 40

HOPE RE-GROWS IN SPRING

No one who trusts in you will ever be disgraced, ... Show me the path where I should walk, Lord; point out the right road for me to follow.

—Psalm 25:3a, 4

H*ope* is a rather wimpy word in 21st century America. To many people, "I hope" means little more than "I wish."

In the Bible the word *hope* is a hearty, beefed-up word, with the tone of: "I've got my eye on the goal, and I'm not taking it off until I arrive there!" Two components make up hope: one is *assurance,* a firm, trusting grasp of God's promises, and the other is *waiting expectantly.* When you wait expectantly, you are open and poised to be surprised and encouraged. C.S.Lewis wrote a book about the first half of his life, entitled *Surprised by Joy.*

Last year, for the first time, Julie and I bought cut tulips at the supermarket. We had bought tulip plants, but never cut stems, because they looked so all-green. They had buds, but they seemed so dormant, without a promise of blooming.

When we got home that day, we put the cut stems in a green glass vase with a few grains of Miracle Grow. We set them on the dining room table and went to bed. Next morning when we walked into the dining room for breakfast, the tulip blooms had burst into beauty. Red tulips lit up our pale green tablecloth.

When the flowers broke out of their "cocoon," they jump-started our hopes with their fresh loveliness. God has many joyful surprises waiting for Christian married people. God loves to throw surprise parties. His purpose is to beef up our trust and hope in Christ. Eugene Peterson and Dean Nadasdy (I minister with him in Woodbury, Minnesota) have devised an equation for hope: Faith + Imagination = Hope. (The corollary is also true: Doubt + Imagination = Worry.)

Let's apply: St. Paul encouraged the Philippians to focus their imagination on: "whatever is noble, whatever is pure, whatever is lovely" (4:8). Dr. Karl Menninger, the famous psychiatrist and founder of the Menninger Clinic in Topeka, Kansas, was once asked what he would do if he was sad and lonely, with that feeling of empty void, and fearful about his own mental state. He replied, "I would stop what I was doing and go help someone." Try it. Do some small act of kindness for a member of your family or someone else.

Let's pray: Dear Lord our God, thank you for every beautiful image, each positive activity with which you cleanse and recycle our hopes. Protect us from nursing unsavory thoughts and attitudes, which intimidate our hearts with helplessness. Move us to open the windows of our eyes, minds, and hearts to the signs of new life all around us. Thank you for the rest your Word provides us, for the opportunity to meet with you daily. Thank you for the full hope we have in Christ. Amen.

CHAPTER 41

FRAGRANCE OF GOD

IN YOUR HOME

The voice of the turtledove is heard in our land. The fig tree puts forth
its figs, and the vines are in blossom; they give forth fragrance.
—The Song of Solomon 2:12 (RSV)

A s the passage above from The Song of Solomon says, we not
only hear spring sounds: "the voice of the turtledove is heard."
We also smell rich aromas: "the vines give forth fragrance." The
return of spring evokes an aura of the time we fell in love with the one
who is now our husband or wife.

The smell of fig trees in the spring invites us to taste the delicious
fruit. Though the agricultural setting of the land of Israel three thousand years ago differs from ours in some respects, our minds can easily
visualize the beauty of spring.

Almost all of us want to have homes that not only look becoming,
but also exude an aroma that invites guests to enter and relax. We want
to enjoy our homes, and we also do not want to be embarrassed when
friends come to call. A home of delicious aromas announces: "Love and
joy live here."

Our senses work together to present us with a total esthetic experience: the *sounds* of birds sing their happiness that spring has returned.
The *smells* of blossoming trees assure us that this year's growth in the

biological world has begun. These stimuli prove to us that we can trust the signals our senses communicate to us.

Scientists have studied which of the five senses (sight, hearing, smell, taste, or touch) our bodies trust most. The sense of smell was the winner. We trust our olfactory nerves more implicitly than the other four senses, they tell us, because sense of *smell* seems to lie to us least often. Even our sense of taste gets help from her sister sense of smell. Our tongue is only able to distinguish four broad tastes: sweet, sour, salty, and bitter. The final taste-test is done by our nose. We "smell" various tastes inside our noses, enabling us to enjoy thousands of tastes.

You open the door of your garage and drive in, closing the door on a demanding day of work. You open the kitchen door as the heavenly fragrance of just-baked banana bread envelops you. Walking into the kitchen, you *see* your wife or husband grasp a bread pan from the oven. You *hear* the gentle clap of the bread pan on the cooling rack on the counter. She or he invites, "Like a slice?" You talk about the events of your mutual day as the banana bread cools. She or he cuts a piece. You enjoy the soft moist *feel* of the bread. You are *home.*

Let's apply: We know that the enjoyment of our senses, while very pleasurable, is not something we should idolize apart from the giver. Take each sense in turn and thank God for the gifts he gives us of our *hearing, seeing, smelling, tasting, touching.*

Let's pray together: Thank you, dear Creator Lord, for all you've given to enrich our lives. You not only made us from scratch, you also use a myriad of means to nourish our whole persons. As you feed and fuel our bodies, minds, and spirits, you strengthen us to live for you. You give us the strength and willing motivation to serve people with your love. Thank you for keeping our praises pure, free from idolatry. In Jesus. Amen.

CHAPTER 42

WHAT DOES LIFE SMELL LIKE?

Our lives are a fragrance presented by Christ to God. But this fragrance is perceived differently by those being saved and by those perishing. To those who are perishing we are a fearful smell of death and doom. But to those who are being saved we are a life-giving perfume.

—2 Corinthians 2:15–16

What does your life *smell* like? What is the aroma of your life and your marriage? What kind of atmosphere do people perceive when they're around you?

Most people love the smell of babies. It's not a heavy, but a subtle, fresh, and sweet aroma. And their breath! They've even named a flowering plant after it: baby's breath. The smell of babies is the smell of new life.

The verse above says that God, who knows everything, considers us to have the aroma of Christ clinging to us, the unmistakable fragrance of the Savior himself alive and present in our lives. "We are to God the aroma of Christ." Paul says that, depending on their spiritual condition, people may perceive us in one of two very contrasting ways: We are either the aroma of life or the smell of death, depending on where they're coming from.

To those who know God and believe him—Paul identifies them as "those who are being saved"—believers smell like roses. They have the fragrance of new life, fresh and inviting, like that which arises from a newborn baby. Those who are inclined toward God are edified by being around other believers, while those who are spiritually dying have a different impression. They can't get away from believers fast enough.

Some disagree that God gives us the responsibility to "smell nice" to people. Touting their independence, they argue, "I don't see why we need to concern ourselves with what people think of us," as if it's presumptuous to think we need to reflect God to people.

God does place into our hands the privilege and responsibility of doing our best to influence people for Christ. The interesting thing is that our perceptions can change. Have you ever met someone whom you disliked at first, perhaps even intensely? Later on, by working through the issues and getting to know him or her, your initial dislike turned into avid interest—or even love. When you were dating your spouse, did that happen? Things about him or her you didn't like at first, changed. And now you *love* her/his aroma?

Let's apply: Honestly, how do people think of you as a couple, people who have known you for a little while? What kind of aroma arises from the two of you?

Let's pray together: We pray, Lord, that there are some who, though at first don't think much of us, afterwards come to see a reflection of your love emanating from us, and eventually come to trust Jesus themselves. May our witness of you be fragrant, refreshing, and authentic. In Jesus, who daily gives us opportunities to pass on the refreshing breeze of your love. Amen.

CHAPTER 43

FROM LISTLESS

TO LOVING

And everything you do must be done with love.
—1 Corinthians 16:14

And whatever you do or say let it be as a representative of the Lord Jesus, all the while giving thanks through him to God the Father.
—Colossians 3:17

There are times when we feel *listless*. It may happen when we are recovering from an illness or surgery, or when we've had unexpected car repair expenses, or an appliance has broken down, or we've been laid off from our job. Or we've worked hard on a project that didn't work out. Or our marriage doesn't seem to be moving ahead—at least for now.

God has wired us humans to function best when we're able to set clear goals and are actively moving toward reaching them. Don't be discouraged if once in a while a thought arises to the effect that it might be easier to give up. Thoughts of this nature arise periodically in almost everyone. This is not clinical depression, but rather a case of "the blahs."

To fuel your patience, count your blessings daily. Meditate on the person and presence of God and all he has done on your behalf. Make a list of the benefits God is providing you and your family. Add to the list additional benefits as you receive new gifts from God.

The words from 1 Corinthians and Colossians point out both the *goal* for our life, and the *style* we are to display as we move toward our goal. "Doing everything . . . as a representative of the Lord Jesus, giving thanks to God" reveals our *goal*: living and working to please God. "And everything you do must be done with love" (our *style* is the very love we've received from God).

Love produces unity between the two of us who are united in Christ. We hold common goals, arising out of the vision God provides us. As a couple in Christ, our marriage is a microcosm of Christ's body, the church. Connected to Christ our head, she and I (he and I) are his body members, designed by God to work in a loving, coordinated way as he directs.

At times we sense some dissonance in our relationship. Our coordinated living and working become temporarily listless. Listen as the apostle Paul stimulates us with words of encouragement: "Give thanks to God the Father. Whatever you do or say, do it as a representative of the Lord Jesus. Do everything [including cleaning the bathroom] in love." We receive renewed energy, and our imagination receives a new spark. We become more confident of God's forgiveness. Our joy begins to return.

Let's apply: For this exercise, I have separate assignments for each of you. For the one who feels listless lately: As you go about your normal activities, slow your pace a little. Start and finish each physical movement deliberately, not jerky. Slow down your walking, eating—each action you take during the day. You may have the perception that you're living in slow motion. Don't worry, just keep moving; for you are trading haste and speed for being able to continue doing the activities important to you. Act *as if* your life is normal, and before long it will be. For the other spouse: Strengthen your husband or wife by encouraging him or her for each day lived faithfully for the Lord and each other. And remember that at some later time, your roles may switch and you might become the one feeling temporarily listless.

Let's pray together: Spirit of God, please rescue us off any islands of isolation. Thank you for your loving Word, which helps us fit the pieces of our life into a coordinated pattern. The gift of your Word is our energy source and central organizing principle. Thus we see the dust of listlessness being swept out of our spirit. Thank you for renewing us with even small measures of joyful enthusiasm. Thank you for reaffirming the purpose of our life: to *please you*. Thank you for empowering us and our actions in the style of your Son, doing everything in *love*. In Jesus, Amen.

CHAPTER 44

HANDICAPPED
ACCESSIBLE

Christ has brought us into this place of highest privilege (grace) where we now stand . . . . We can rejoice, too, when we run into problems and trials, for we know that they are good for us—they help us learn to endure. And endurance develops strength of character in us, and character strengthens our confident expectation of salvation.

—Romans 5:2–5

When we got married we received each other with "warts and all." We all have warts, of course. We promised, "I take you to be my husband, wife . . . for better, for worse, for richer, for poorer, in sickness and in health, to love and to cherish . . . ."

The question is not whether the person we're marrying has factors that detract from our ideal image of him or her. The question is how we *perceive* and treat each other with those less-than-perfect elements. We all, bar none, are "handicapped" in some way: physically, spiritually, emotionally, visibly, or invisibly.

Our country has seen great strides in helping make life workable for those with physical disabilities. We have handicap accessible curbs, doors, and toilets. The Congress has passed the ADA Act (Americans with Disability Act). It stipulates that employers must provide working conditions for people with disabilities so they can function and accomplish their job goals.

In order to receive the benefits of that law, workers have to admit and validate that they have a disability. That's even more true in marriage. Are we willing to acknowledge we have shortcomings that at times form obstacles to our total performance? If so, we can avoid isolating, or being isolated, as "the one with the problem." Admitting our sin and our mutual need for God's help is step one toward an honest and loving marital relationship. Step two is constantly appreciating our status under God, that we are covered by his grace and forgiveness, justified in God's sight by what Christ did for us.

Paul outlines a four-step process for understanding and accepting our hard times:

1. We rejoice in our *sufferings*.
2. We know that suffering produces *perseverance,* staying power.
3. While we persevere, God develops our *character*.
4. People in whom God develops character, have *hope*. They hold on.

Wives and husbands who are hope-filled are more generous in accepting and forgiving each other. They generously share their love with each other. They have a strong sense that God makes his help available to them and each other, as needs arise, on a daily basis.

Let's apply: In what circumstances have you discovered that God's forgiveness and the gifts of the Holy Spirit are vastly more valuable for your life than houses, cars, bank accounts, and investments?

Let's pray together: Together speak the words of this hymn: "O Holy Spirit, enter in, and in our hearts your work begin, and make our hearts your dwelling." Amen.

CHAPTER 45

HUMOR AND LOVE

. . . What counts is whether we really have been changed into new and different people.

—Galatians 6:15

"Laughter is internal jogging," Rich Bimler, president of Wheat Ridge Ministries, said in a speech I heard. Laughter shakes our body, jiggling loose our tensions and pretensions. It frees us to regain our balance of joy and responsibility, seriousness and lightheartedness. A well-distributed balance of joy and responsibility helps us married folks not get tipped over by our troubles.

A little healthy humor can do wonders for our homes and our marriages. Some individuals have the knack of noticing contrasts, incongruities, and absurdities in life, and then pointing them out in a few, succinct words. People around them laugh gratefully. Often all we need is a short joke to lift us out of heaviness, enabling us to change our mood and redistribute the weight of our responsibilities—or at least our perception of them. The appropriate use of humor can help us to balance the issues in our life so we can avoid undue worry and glumness.

What kind of humor do you use in your family? Sarcastic humor is often counter-productive. Self-deprecating humor is usually safe, because we poke fun at our own mistakes and foibles, without pointing the finger of criticism at others.

G. K. Chesterton said, "Angels can fly because they take themselves lightly. Never forget that Satan fell by force of 'gravity'." Some folks justify their negativism by claiming that they're "just being realistic." In truth, it may be "force of gravity" or heaviness that is weighing us down. Instead, let's be like the angels, taking ourselves lightly and letting ourselves receive welcome measures of buoyancy, resiliency, and joy from God.

Let's apply: Before a word of humor leaves your lips, ask yourself, "Am I using this humor to attract attention to myself or to manipulate her or him to do something I want done? Am I using my attempt at humor to expose his or her weakness? Am I perhaps being cruel?" Read Ephesians 4:29 (NIV) twice out loud, and discuss its implications: "Do not let any unwholesome talk come out of your mouths, but only what is helpful for building others up according to their needs, that it may benefit those who listen."

Let's pray together: Gracious Father, help us see laughable contrasts in nature and life around us, so we may receive your gifts of lightness, grace, and balance. You must get a chuckle out of our pretensions, hangups, and over-seriousness, even as you forgive and restore us. Protect us from taking ourselves too seriously, or making requests of each other that are actually thinly-disguised demands. Help us at all times to have a word of forgiveness prepared and ready to give each other. In Christ we pray. Amen.

CHAPTER 46

LAUGHTER ALL AROUND

Blessed are you who weep now, for you will laugh.

—Luke 6:21b

When Julie's and my children were small and she would see them teasing each other too much, she would remind them, "It's only funny if everyone is laughing." This is a helpful truth for us adults as well.

Let's make it our goal to please the Holy Spirit by the way we talk and act, beginning with what strikes us as funny. Paul urged us in Ephesians 4:30 not to grieve the Holy Spirit. So it follows that it's possible to please him. God surely takes pleasure when we experience loving laughter, which loosens our bonds of anxiety and worry.

I read somewhere that children smile forty-five times an hour and laugh every seven and a half minutes. I wonder what our score as adults might be.

James Thurber wrote, "Humor is emotional chaos remembered in times of tranquility."

Joy looks forward to the future and provides us with a perspective that is a little like amnesia; it helps us forget the pain of the past, especially pain that is better buried. Football great Walter Payton was the running back of the Chicago Bears when they played in the Super Bowl a few years ago. It took him eleven seasons as a pro and an unsurpassed 14,860 rushing yards to make it.

After winning the game that qualified the Bears for the Super Bowl, Payton was asked about the bad times he had experienced during those eleven years. "No bad times," he said. "Can't even think about bad times. Hey, are you sure there were any?"

What an attitude to have in our married life! In thinking of the past years of our married life, what if we could say, "Can't even think about bad times. Are you sure there were any?"

Let's apply: Among your group of friends and acquaintances, which ones make you laugh? Plan to go out with them and prepare to have a fun evening.

Let's pray together: Dear Lord Jesus, help us forget what we need to forget and remember what we need to remember—especially your good promises and the wonderful ways you enrich our lives every day. Thank you for the people who lift us with their warm, interesting humor and positive attitudes. Amen.

CHAPTER 47

RINGS AND PIES

All of you, live in harmony with one another . . . be compassionate and humble.

—1 Peter 3:8

It takes personal humility and a hearty sense of compassion to live in harmony with our family and community. These twin attributes of humility and compassion are suggested in the graphics below, the entwined wedding rings and the pie graph.

Remember the moment during your wedding when you exchanged rings? In Christian symbolism, *rings* express eternal life with God our Savior, and the enduring quality of a strong marital relationship. The *pie graph* visualizes the four important relational components of our lives: God, Family, Work, and Community.

After the jeweler melted the gold, silver, or platinum to make your rings, the seam was no longer visible. Well-made rings have no beginning and no end. Some couples, after being married for some years, can be heard to say: "It seems like we've been married a lot longer than the number of our years." A good sign.

The four pieces of the pie graph illustrate our four main roles/relationships in this world. Because we are still fallible human beings, we all make mistakes in all four areas. God calls us to be faithful in each area, fulfilling our responsibilities and living in harmony with the people with whom we share our life.

Try as we might, though, we all regularly fall short. We struggle with the temptation to over-emphasize *my rights* over *yours*. Because of our sinfulness, we may compete with others over whose rights will come out on top when there is a conflict.

Or we may become so fixated on our involvement in one of the four areas, that we do a disservice to people in the other three. Ultimately, we are responsible to God as his stewards in all four areas of our lives. And as a married couple, we can help each other faithfully to live out our stewardship life under him.

For example, I may become so engrossed in my work that I neglect my personal relationship with God and the members of my family. God created us to live in community with each other, beginning with our spouses. Let's ask God to help us especially to avoid leaving our families with "the short end of the stick."

Let's apply: Being honest, each of you, ask yourself: In which of my four roles/relationships (God, family, work, community) am I the strongest? Weakest? How can I strengthen the weakest link? How can I correct the imbalances, if I am focusing an inordinate amount of my attention in one area?

Let's pray together: Please forgive us, dear Lord, for allowing our egos to fall in love with our role/relationships in one of the four areas, to the detriment of the other three. Mellow our pride and help us use our time and resources wisely, so that, in consultation with each other, we can arrive at a good, harmonious pace in our lifestyle. Give us courage when it's time to make decisions in these matters, including when to say yes and when to say no. Amen.

CHAPTER 48

PROJECTING

OUR FEELINGS

If we are unfaithful, God remains faithful, for he cannot deny himself.

—2 Timothy 2:13

In the passage above Paul speaks the truth that God never projects bad feelings onto us. Even when we are unfaithful to him, God still remains faithful. He is never petulant or pouty. He has total integrity. "He cannot deny himself."

But we may project our negative feelings onto other people, especially our spouse, and onto God as well.

In trying to understand each other, we probe beneath the surface to understand where the other is coming from. But instead of thinking objectively about our partner, we may harbor negative feelings that we inaccurately ascribe to him or her: "What you're really thinking is. . . . The reason you are looking at it that way is . . . ." When we project such negative emotions onto our partner, he or she will feel unfairly treated and our oneness will take a blow.

We may even project our negative feelings onto God. When we become ill, we may complain, "What does God have against me, that I've gotten sick like this?" The good news is that God is not like us humans. He does not harbor hurt feelings and waves of changeable emotions.

Look at the passage above again. It describes God's "broad shoulders" of understanding. He remains strong and objective even when we waver: "If we are unfaithful, he remains faithful, for he cannot deny himself."

God will keep on loving us, remaining gracious and ready to forgive us, no matter how we misunderstand him. He is ready to receive us back and help us become reconciled to him. He will help us grow out of projecting our feelings. His Holy Spirit will guide us to understand and trust our Father and each other.

Let's apply: Being very honest and transparent, admit to each other at least one time when you projected your negative feelings onto God, each other, or both. How can you avoid doing that in the future?

Let's pray together: Gracious God, thanks for your Holy Spirit who helps me know you as you really are—not fickle but genuine, not unreliable but dependable, full of complete understanding and deepest love toward us. We trust you, our true God, for Jesus' sake. Amen.

CHAPTER 49

FINE COLLECTIBLES

The Kingdom of Heaven is like a treasure that a man discovered hidden in a field. In his excitement, he hid it again and sold everything he owned to get enough money to buy the field—and get the treasure, too!

—Matthew 13:44–45

Antique aficionados enjoy the quest for objects of beauty and value from the past, things that have lasted. On finding a treasured item—perhaps at an unexpected time or in an out-of-the-way place—they experience a burst of joy.

It's fun to collect things, whether it is old gold, baseball cards, dolls, kitchen utensils, blue glass, dishes, coins, or stamps. The joy of the quest continues, and the thrill is savored not only at the time it's discovered and purchased, but long afterward.

Jesus spoke of such a quest in the passage above. The happy discoverer is very willing to pay a high price to purchase the treasure. He knows the exchange will be to his clear advantage.

Christian counselor Don Beiswenger quoted the founder of Holiday Inn motels: "In the hotel business it's all about location, location, location." Beiswenger changed it to: "In life and in families it's all about relationships, relationships, relationships." Establishing a marriage and family built on a solid foundation of trust and love is like discovering a valuable collectible that many search for all their lives—and some never find.

Some couples or individuals don't discover the great value of their faith and a loving marriage until they encounter a crisis, an accident, or a serious illness. After the crisis is over, many are deeply thankful to have discovered the value of the relationship sooner rather than later, while there was still time for reconciliation and healing. With warm gratefulness they say, "If that's what it took to open my eyes, that's all right. I could have lost her or him completely."

Let's apply: What is the most valuable material collectible you possess? In the spiritual and relational realm, who is your most valuable asset? Have you understood his or her value long ago, more recently through a crisis event, or has your appreciation grown steadily over the years?

Let's pray together: Lord Jesus, in you I have found the source of joy in my life, my greatest treasure. Help me generously to share you and your love with my husband or wife, family, and friends. Amen.

CHAPTER 50

SELF-STYLED
CELEBRATIONS

I will bless the LORD who guides me; even at night my heart instructs me. I know the LORD is always with me. I will not be shaken, for he is right beside me.

—Psalm 16:7–8

There are inner celebrations and outer celebrations. Outer celebrations are holidays that have been determined by church and society, like Christmas and Easter, Memorial Day and July 4th, Labor Day and Thanksgiving Day. These celebrations help all of us, giving us permission to relax. Because the whole community is on holiday, no one needs to fear being perceived by others as lazy.

Inner celebrations are ones that we as a family decide to hold, for our own reasons. We celebrate at regulated times like birthdays and anniversaries. We can also design our own family celebrations whenever we wish. You could call these "celebrations of the heart." If you've recovered from serious illness, your loved ones may plan a dinner to celebrate, when everyone gathers to thank God for the gift of your regained health.

A third kind of celebration might be called a personal thank-you celebration, a party all by oneself. For example, we might get up in the middle of the night and thank God for guiding us safely to the resolution of a problem that was vexing us. Though we usually wake up at night because our body can't relax, there are times we just feel excited and sleepless for joy.

At such times, I get up very quietly, so I don't wake my wife. I pour a bowl of cereal and eat it sitting in the Lay-Z-Boy chair in our front room. I breathe deep thanks to God for guiding me through a narrow place on my life-road, and read words like: "I will bless the Lord who guides me; even at night my heart instructs me. I know the Lord is always with me. I will not be shaken, for he is right beside me" (Psalm 16:7–8). I admire the cut flowers that grace our dining room table. As I say Amen to his goodness and crawl back into bed, I feel grateful to my heavenly Father for his help, and for my sleeping family. Great contentment covers me like the comforter I pull up to my chin.

Let's apply: On paper (it's a good idea to set up a notebook to record such things), recall two incidents in which God rescued you or a member of your family. At the end of each notation write, "Thank you, Lord."

Let's pray together: Pray with the inspired words of Psalm 4:7–8, "You have given me greater joy than those who have abundant harvests of grain and wine. I will lie down in peace and sleep, for you alone, O Lord, will keep me safe." Good night, Father. Amen.

CHAPTER 51

CLOSER THAN A BROTHER,

CLOSER THAN A SISTER

By the grace of God I am what I am.

—1 Corinthians 15:10

N ext only to our relationship with God, our bond as husband and wife is the most intimate in this life. Proverbs describes certain friends being closer than siblings: "There is a friend who sticks closer than a brother" (18:24, NIV). Adam referred to his wife Eve in closer terms yet: "At last!" Adam exclaimed. "She is part of my own flesh and bone! She will be called 'woman,' because she was taken out of a man" (Genesis 2:23).

Paul goes further still, urging, "You husbands must love your wives with the same love Christ showed the church. He gave up his life for her to make her holy . . ." (Ephesians 5:25–26a).

Being in this close relationship places us in a position of high responsibility, with the ability to influence each other's life for good or ill. We can either help strengthen each other's faith and love, or contribute to each other's disillusionment. We can either help firm up each other's hope in God, or sap each other's confidence in God and our ability to love.

Because God entrusts us with such high responsibility for each other, he often raises the bar of challenge above our comfort level. Many times during our married life we struggle, thinking: "I'm not sure I can handle this by myself. It's just too difficult." I'm convinced that when God allows us to hit the wall of our limitations, he never does it with mixed motives, but only with the most loving purpose in mind. He leads us gently to admit we're helpless without him. We can only rely on our dear Lord to help us out.

God smiles: "I thought you'd never ask." He assures us he's more than pleased to work with us, making good use of our weaknesses as well as our strengths, as his tools.

Let's apply: Psychologists tell us that we humans live in fulfilled relationships when we have access to both parts of our *personas,* both our "masculine" and "feminine" sides, strengths, and skills. How do we see both kinds of strength functioning in ourselves as individuals and as a couple?

Let's pray together: Dear Lord God, you have graciously bonded us as a couple in Christ. Help us to grow in your grace together, "till death parts us." In Christ. Amen.

CHAPTER 52

CHILDREN OF THE RESURRECTION-I

A devotion addressed to parents who have lost a child

> Those who are considered worthy of taking part in that age and in the resurrection from the dead . . . can no longer die; for they are like the angels. They are God's children because they are children of the resurrection.
>
> —Luke 20:3–36

May God comfort you with the sure and certain hope you have in Christ. He lived, died, and rose again in order to give your child the gift of forgiveness and eternal life. Jesus assures you that, living or dying, God's angels attend your children: "I tell you that *their angels* always see the face of my Father in heaven" (Matthew 18:10, NIV).

Jesus clearly revealed how God feels about children. One day some parents brought their children to Jesus, asking him to bless them. The disciples became huffy and tried to turn them away. The Savior zinged the disciples for their attitude, and gave the little ones the blessing they came for. He took them in his arms and said, "Let the children come to me. Do not stop them! For the kingdom of God belongs to such as these" (Mark 10:14).

Jesus said believers are "considered worthy of taking part in . . . the resurrection from the dead." They are "God's children because they are children of the resurrection." Paul wrote, "We died, and were buried with Christ by baptism. And just as Christ was raised from the dead by the glorious power of the Father, now we also may live new lives" (Romans 6:4).

We—and your child—have come to trust Christ and received the gift of eternal life. Thus already during our life here we have begun to live that "new resurrected life" by faith. This is our first spiritual resurrection. Meanwhile, we look forward to the second resurrection when Jesus returns. Then he'll reunite our bodies with our souls. Then you will see your child again. Then we'll enjoy all the blessings of heaven forever.

When God allowed your child to be transferred from this life, she or he became "like an angel." Your child has already begun to enjoy that fulfilled promise.

[Note to you readers who have not lost a child: While this and the next devotion do not apply to you at this time, I have three reasons for inviting you to read them: 1. For the future possibility—God willing it will not happen—that you should lose a child. 2. Losing a child places a great deal of stress on a couple's marriage. 3. To help you understand more deeply what grieving parents go through, so you may comfort them. Following these two devotions addressed to grieving parents, you will see three devotions addressed to this very issue, to help you, their friends, provide the most appropriate comfort you can for your grieving friends.]

Let's apply: It may be hard to imagine the time when your tears will stop. Reflect on and discuss these words from Psalm 126:5–6, "Those who plant in tears will harvest with songs of joy. They weep as they go to plant their seed, but they sing as they return with the harvest."

Let's pray together: O Lord of life and conqueror of death, we come into your presence with our tears still flowing. Thank you for acknowledging our grief. Thank you for understanding us and holding our broken hearts in your hands. Please sustain us and see us through this time. We pray in the name of Jesus, of whom Isaiah said, "Surely he has borne our griefs and carried our sorrows" (Isaiah 53:4, RSV). Amen.

CHAPTER 53

CHILDREN OF THE RESURRECTION-II

A devotion addressed to those who have lost a child

God is not God of the dead, but of the living, for to him all are alive.

—Luke 20:38 (NIV)

Nothing can ever separate us from his love . . . death can't, and life can't. Our fears for today, our worries about tomorrow . . . nothing in all creation will ever be able to separate us from the love of God that is revealed in Christ Jesus our Lord.

—Romans 8:37–39

What wonderful joys you'll have when you greet your child on the other side. But meanwhile, you may struggle with questions such as: Is our relationship with God still intact? Since our child passed away, has God distanced himself from us, or is this just our perception?

In the Bible, sins are divided into two groups: sins of *commission*, where we do what God tells us not to do; and sins of *omission*, where we fail to do some positive action God asks us to do. Following the death of a loved one, our hardest struggle is usually about our imagined sins of omission.

The evil one suggests questions such as: Did we love our child *enough?* Did we do *enough* to express our love to him or her? Could we have done something else to keep him or her from dying? These questions are in the realm of the hypothetical, which, like a vacuum, can suck us into a void where we question God's love and our faith. Imagined sins of omission can undermine our trust in God and our confidence regarding our status as his children. Or they can cause subtle suspicions toward our spouse to fester. Such thoughts can turn into silent accusations that drive a wedge between us.

God's mercy and love are accessible to both of us: "The Lord is close to the brokenhearted; he rescues those who are crushed in spirit" (Psalm 34:18). God's forgiveness is available to us at all times: "You are already clean because of the Word I have spoken to you" (John 15:3, NIV).

Look at the passages above. The first one affirms that God is equally alive with us who are still on this earth, as well as with those whom he has released to heaven: "God is not God of the dead, but of the living, for to him all are alive." The second passage affirms that no obstacle can block "the love of God that is revealed in Christ Jesus our Lord" from coming to us.

Let's apply: Watch for any—even small—seeds and weeds of imagined guilt inside yourself or your spouse in regard to your child who has passed away. Encourage each other at all times to accept God's loving promises.

Let's pray together: Dear Father, thank you for assuring us you have totally wiped clean our misdeeds of both omission and commission. We look to you to rebuild our hopes and confidence. We trust that Christ did everything necessary to make things right with you. Heal our broken hearts in ways only you can. In Jesus, who loves our family. Amen.

CHAPTER 54

HOW TO SHARE
COMFORT-I

Devotion to help you comfort friends who have lost a child

All praise to the God and Father of our Lord Jesus Christ. He is the source of every mercy and the God who comforts us. He comforts us in all our troubles so that we can comfort others (with) the same comfort God has given us.

—2 Corinthians 1:3–4

My brother phoned to tell me his six-year-old grandson had died of leukemia. He said, "It feels like our family has suffered a great setback."

A setback—some have described grief as being like a blow that knocks the wind out of you. Other parents say after the death of their child: "It's all wrong. I should have preceded my child in death, not the other way around." Or: "I wish it had been *me* instead of my child." How do you bring comfort to moms and dads who have experienced such indescribable pain in their hearts and souls?

First, re-establish your relationship with them. Pray to your heavenly Father for opportunities to spend time with them. Give them quiet assurance that you are there primarily to be at their side. Convey that you are available to carry a portion of their load. Ask them to be very honest when they need time to be alone.

Second, be ready to listen when they want to talk about their child. Theologian Paul Tillich said, "The first duty of love is to listen." Don't advise, hurry, or finish their sentences for them. Relax together, sharing peaceful communication that doesn't necessarily need words. When they are able to talk about their departed little loved one, let them "call the shots." This will help them in a number of ways. Among them, it will help allay their fear that their child might be forgotten.

Let's apply: Think of specific ways you can be of help. For example, offer to babysit their other children so they can go on errands, see a movie, or eat at a restaurant. Prepare and take over some supper meals, especially in the first days after the funeral. I have known some friends who cooked three or four meals, froze them, and brought them over, so the family could eat them whenever it was convenient for them.

Let pray together: Dear Lord, we remember the time we had a death in our family, and others came to our side. Empower us now that it's our turn to help. Amen.

CHAPTER 55

How to Share
Comfort-II

A devotion to help you share God's comfort
with friends who've lost a child

Day and night, I have only tears for food . . .

—Psalm 42:3

God himself will be with them. He will remove all their sorrows, and there will be no more death or sorrow or crying or pain. For the old world and all its evils are gone forever.

—Revelation 21:4–5

Tears. Many tears flow when we grieve, especially parents who have lost a child. As the writer of Psalm 42 said, there may be times when we cry so much it seems the tears have taken the place of our regular food. At times, something may suddenly remind the parents of their lost child, and tears erupt like an explosion.

We want to be there to comfort them, but we fear we might intrude in their grief and make things worse. We can still be of assistance to them. We may be moved to tears ourselves. Weep with them, whether you're a man or a woman. Sometimes tears express more than words. We may be at a loss what to say. Relax. With words, quietness, or tears, join them in their grieving.

When it's time to say goodbye, it may occur to you to say, "If you need anything, just call." We may forget that to invite them to "just call"—to take the initiative and ask for help—is the very thing that grieving people have difficulty doing. Instead, think about what they *might* need. Think of some small assistance to smooth a rough spot in their day. Think creatively. For example, you could invite them to a low-key gathering at your church, the kind where they can sit in the background, enjoying the peaceful comfort of just being with others.

Let's apply: Discuss: What would *we* want people to do for us, if we experienced such a loss? At home pray together—perhaps aloud—for your grieving friends. Praying for them tends to "prime the pump" of your imagination regarding ways to help them. You can use a prayer like this one:

Let's pray together: Gracious God, by your Spirit inform our spirits so that we can understand our friends' grief in some small but real way. When we share words of comfort and strength with them, enable us to say the kind of words *you* would say, dear Lord. Give us peace in our spirits. Preserve us from becoming impatient, trying to hurry our help. We pray in Jesus, who totally understands both them and us. Amen.

CHAPTER 56

HOW TO SHARE
COMFORT-III

A devotion to help you share God's comfort
with friends who've lost a child

When others are happy, be happy with them. If they are sad, share
their sorrow.

—Romans 12:15

This devotion could be subtitled: "Pray for Strength in their Marriage."

One day I heard a grief counselor explain that couples who've lost a child are more vulnerable to strain in their marriage. Their rates of divorce are higher than average. Why? One factor is whether they grieve together or separately.

Remember the words in a previous devotion addressed to parents who have lost a child: "Watch for any—even small—seeds and weeds of imagined guilt in regard to your child who passed away." People grieve in a variety of ways. One parent may struggle with feelings of imagined guilt, while the other may tend to blame his or her partner. Either way, the strength and stability of their marriage may be threatened.

Here are some ideas to include in your prayers for such a beloved couple:

1. Pray for them to be able to grieve *together,* not separately. Satan will try to drive a wedge of guilt or blame between them. Often it revolves around real or imagined sins of omission previously referred to.
2. Pray for them to grow in faith and trust in their Savior even while they are grieving. Ask God the Holy Spirit to help them accept themselves as imperfect human beings who, like all of us, are totally dependent on God for his grace. Pray that when one is grieving, the other will lift up him or her. Another day they will switch roles. Assure them that this phenomenon is very normal.
3. Pray for them to derive all possible benefits from worship and the Lord's Supper. God will assure them that they do not bear their burdens alone. One of the main reasons God groups believers together in his "body" the church is to make us available to each other, especially when part of our body is reeling from a death in the family. Paul wrote, "We all eat from one loaf, showing that we are one body." (1 Corinthians 10:17).

Let's apply: Help each other know the worthwhileness of this ministry of standing together with those who are grieving: "So don't get tired of doing what is good. Don't get discouraged and give up, for we will reap a harvest of blessing at the appropriate time" (Galatians 6:9).

Let's pray together: Dear Father in heaven, thank you for allowing us the privilege to be loving friends of our brother and sister who lost their precious child. Every day help them rest their grieving hearts in your merciful promises. Protect them and their marriage by your strong, comforting Holy Spirit during days of special vulnerability. In Christ we pray, believing. Amen.

CHAPTER 57

WHILE YOU'RE
ON VACATION-I

Jesus said, "Come, be my disciples, and I will show you how to fish for people!"

—Mark 1:17

Vacation time!

One way you and your family can refresh yourselves and recycle your energies is by changing your environment, at least for a few days. Trips and vacations can rejuvenate your bodies, your emotions, and your spirits. They provide a time to review the ways you're expending your energies, and perhaps do a "mid-course adjustment" of the direction your life is taking.

Many people—especially here in Minnesota—love to recreate their energies by fishing. There are many species of fish that are caught in our 15,000 lakes. Fishermen employ their creative energies to decide what bait or lure will appeal to which kind of fish. Jesus promises, "I will show you how to fish for people." Jesus is reminding us not to get stuck on our own needs and comforts, but to extend our interests and energies for the benefit of people and their eternal outcome.

Jesus called his first four disciples, Peter and Andrew, James and John, while they were working as professional fishermen. He invited them to become part of his group of disciples: "Come, be my disciples, and I will show you how to fish for people!" He invited them to change their vocation from commercial fishing to become God's agents, helping gather people into the net of God's love.

While Jesus called each one of them personally, he assembled them into a group of believers. He trained them to share God's love freely with people, inviting as many folks as possible to receive what God had lavishly prepared for them: forgiveness, grace, joy, love, and eternal life. Just as Jesus gave them eternal life as a gift, so they were to extend the invitation to people without cost. Fishing for people cannot be done without loving them. Both require stepping outside ourselves to engage and relate to people according to their actual needs.

Two married people live in a bond of love and mutual caring not unlike our bond as members of Christ's body the church. If we are to be truly united in love, we need to have common goals and aspirations. A woman and man who are united in God's love, will extend themselves to others, sharing a portion of that lavish love they themselves have received from God.

Let's apply: Say a prayer of thanks to God for sending people into your life who led you to Christ. Whether it was your parents or others, you would not be trusting Christ today if not for those individuals who forgot themselves and unselfishly reached out to you. Write them a note or call them on the phone, expressing your gratefulness to them.

Let's pray together: Call to our minds, dear Lord, specific individuals who are without a relationship with Jesus Christ at this time. We pray for them right now, in the context of their situation and their needs. Create in us a desire to reach out and touch them with a word or a gesture which amounts to *you* inviting them into a deeper relationship with their heavenly Father—and ours. Thank you for this time to recharge our spiritual, physical, and emotional "batteries." Amen.

CHAPTER **58**

WHILE YOU'RE
ON VACATION-II

The Kingdom of Heaven is like a fishing net that is thrown into the
water and gathers fish of every kind. When the net is full, they drag it
up onto the shore, sit down, sort the good fish into crates, and throw
the bad ones away.

—Matthew 13:47–48

Our family forms the most important filter for our values. The
media, teachers, pastors, friends, coworkers, and our society
influence us a great deal. But when it comes to actually deciding on which values we hold high and dear, and which ones we discard,
our family is the main sieve.

Discovering our values is like fishing with a net. The process of
sorting out all the communications we receive every day—including
our perceptions and impressions—is like making value judgments of
which fish we'll keep and which we'll throw back. We decide which are
the valuable "keepers" and which ones aren't worth it.

Let this analogy of net fishing point you to Jesus as our perfect
fisher-person. To be gathered by him, to be valued and loved by him,
to be called his child—that is the treasure beyond every other, on earth
or the universe.

When we know how much God loves us, we believe and trust him,
as individuals and as a married couple. We help each other evaluate all

that we're exposed to. Thankfully we don't need to do this difficult task alone. Together we filter the values which compete for our attention and loyalty.

The time we spend together on vacation provides opportunities to do this filtering calmly, without rushing the process.

Here's our goal: to replace ourselves as the center of our universe and commit ourselves to serving him, the only one worthy of being our center. When we know how incredibly much it cost God to love us—his own Son's life—then we begin to understand what authentic love is. And he's given us His word, which is the "values grid" for assessing what we will invest our life in.

God invites us to join him and each other to do this people fishing. We place on the front burner of our lives whatever pleases him, instead of our own ego. We trust the Holy Spirit to guide us, to "Test everything . . . hold on to what is good. Keep away from every kind of evil" (1 Thessalonians 5:21–22).

Let's apply: Think of your spouse as a real "catch," an inestimable gift from God. Express this to her or him today.

Please pray separately, in your heart: Practice praying to God in the silence of your heart: "Thank you, dear Lord God, for giving me the extraordinary gift of_____and coupling us in holy marriage. Help me always to honor you for the prize, the gift, she/he is to me. May I respect her/him as next only to yourself, our true God. In Jesus Christ, our Lord. Amen.

CHAPTER 59

WHILE YOU'RE

ON VACATION-III

Is anyone thirsty? Come and drink—even if you have no money!
Come, take your choice of wine and milk—it's all free!
—Isaiah 55:1

When our grandchildren sit on the dock at the cottage and drop small chunks of bread into the lake, they love to watch the sunfish swarm to feed on them. It's a real *feeding frenzy.*

For one week each summer our family of eighteen—Julie and I, our children, spouses, and grandchildren—gathers for our vacation in northern Minnesota. We eat our breakfasts and lunches in our separate cabins. Then for supper we line up two picnic tables and all eat together. There is a great quantity of delicious food, enough for everyone.

The scene might be like a feeding frenzy, a *friendly* feeding frenzy. But like a feeding frenzy, there is competition, not for food, but for "air time." We all want to talk and express ourselves, sometimes at the very same moment. Voice levels and excitement rise as we all vie for attention, listening ears, love, and affirmation from the rest of the family.

We live in three different social contexts/times: 1) Time at work. We were hired for a job to be productive, which produces a certain kind of stress. On the other hand, we receive satisfaction in being productive and socializing on the job site. 2) Time alone, otherwise known as solitude.

141

For us believers, we use this time primarily for reading God's Word and praying. As a couple sharing faith and love in Christ, we spend some of our devotional time with each other and some time alone. 3) Time with others, socializing, whether we're with just our spouse, or with another couple or two to eat or recreate together, or in a larger family, like when all 18 of us eat together on vacation.

Different social chemistries are at work in each of those three social environments. God created us having a cluster of many needs, which are filled in various ways in those environments. But we need all three, in varying degrees and times of our lives. An important benefit of being married is that we can monitor each other's needs, noticing whether our spouse is currently deprived (for example, spending too much time working, and too little time alone or recreating with others), or fulfilled and balanced among the three environments.

Since we are all fallible human beings, we will not be completely satisfied when we're in a group, with our spouse, alone, or on the job. The good news is that God gives us grace wherever we are. He never leaves us or forsakes us.

Let's apply: Two strategies for family vacations or gatherings: First, before leaving home, or on the way driving to the gathering place, pray God to bless every person who'll be there. Pray that everyone will receive "air time" to express him- or herself. Second, while together in the family gathering, depend on God to help you to monitor your tongue and avoid gossiping. "Speak the truth in love" (Ephesians 4:15, NIV). If one family member begins to share, especially if they are a little more introverted than others, slow down the pace of excitement and listen well. Resist the urge to dismiss her or his concerns and feelings as of minor importance not worth listening to. Maintain both honest naturalness and genuine joy in being together.

Let's pray together: By your Holy Spirit, O God, may our family time together serve to strengthen and build (not weaken) our family's spiritual health. We rely on you to provide poise, perspective, and joyful peace, strengthening our family as we grow in trust and love for each other. In Christ Jesus, the head of the church and the head of our family. Amen.

CHAPTER 60

WHILE YOU'RE
ON VACATION-IV

A devotion written especially for men

Give all your worries and cares to God, for he cares about what happens to you.

—1 Peter 5:7

L et's go on vacation again. Did you see the Robert Redford movie *A River Runs Through It?* If you enjoyed it as I did, you may recall the scenes where the late afternoon sun provided backlighting for fishing lines waving gently in the summer air.

The lines appeared silver as they looped through the air, wafting in elliptical patterns, causing the gnats to scurry. Those scenes reminded me of our vacation days on Lower Whitefish Lake in the glad company of our family. During those vacation days, God grants me substantial spiritual, emotional, and physical rejuvenation. When I place my plans and pace on hold and relax, I notice that the tone of my voice becomes less strident, easier to listen to, and my family enjoys being with me more.

We can speculate why God gave us fathers the awesome responsibility to serve as thermostats to monitor (helping or hindering) our family's daily peace. Thankfully, God provides us with the resources of love that enable us to fulfill that role. This lyric is from one of the songs in George Gershwin's opera *Porgy and Bess:* "Fish gotta swim and birds gotta fly, but I gotta love one man till I die." Let those lyrics remind you that God is supplying you with all the love you need, through your wife and family.

Set the tone. Gratefully receive God's gift of rest. From that rest receive a renewal of energy and joy with which you can serve God and people. Pass on that rest and peace to your family.

Imagine yourself in your waders, fishing in a well-stocked trout stream. After that, take a nap in a hammock suspended between two large oak trees.

Let's apply: Start now to plan your vacation for next summer. Enjoy the process of preparing. Give careful thought to how you and your wife can make the vacation as meaningful as possible for each member of your family.

Let's pray together: Dear Lord, as we reflect on images of past vacations, we're reminded of how much you love and care for every person in our family. By your Spirit, please guide us to plan our next vacation in such a way that everyone gets the kind of rest he or she needs. In Jesus, who is glad to receive our prayers and deliver them to the Father. Amen.

CHAPTER 61

WHILE YOU'RE
ON VACATION-V

In relationships among the Lord's people, women are not independent of men, and men are not independent of women . . . everything comes from God.

—1 Corinthians 11:11–12

God created us humans to live as part of a family. Through our marriages and families, God provides us many benefits of spiritual, emotional, and material help, support, security, and joy.

Here we are in 21st century America, facing a strong challenge: Because we are involved in so many things, we don't seem to have enough downtime at home together. Though we may be married, we may also be harried.

God wants us to be *interdependent,* living to help fill each other's needs. We don't want to be so *independent* that we don't really need each other. Nor do we want to be *codependent,* relying on each other's approval to the extent that we can't function without it. Couples who are *interdependent* in Christ love each other in practical ways. Each one is strong and compassionate (giving), while accepting spiritual, emotional, and physical help and nourishment from the other (receiving).

We can grow in the joy of discovering new ways to benefit each other. While living and carrying out our responsibilities each day, we also try to anticipate what our spouse *might* need in the coming days. By doing that, we are not abruptly surprised when she or he has a request or need. We can avoid becoming irritated, dismissing the feeling that we're being put upon. We are willing. We are ready. We feel a surge of satisfaction that our timing is in synch. We feel confident that together the two of us can accomplish things more effectively than either of us could alone. We are grateful for the oneness we have in Christ. We have a sense that we're fulfilling God's gracious will together.

Let's apply: Identify two signs that you and your spouse are functioning in healthy, interdependent ways:

1. _____   2. _____

Let's pray together: Thank you, gracious Father, for the Holy Spirit growing us as individuals and as a couple. We are so grateful for the myriad ways you bless and build our marriage. We pray in Christ, our eternal Bridegroom. Amen.

CHAPTER 62

IN STEP, IN SYNCH-I

If we are living now by the Holy Spirit, let us follow the Holy Spirit's leading in every part of our lives.

—Galatians 5:25

My wife, Julie, and I walk two miles a day, which takes 35 to 40 minutes. When we began these walks, it didn't occur to us it might be helpful for us to walk in step. After a couple of months we realized some of the benefits. Walking in step just works better. The cadence makes the miles and minutes march by faster.

Walking in step feels more secure. We don't need to worry about who's leading and who's following. Turning 90 degree corners, though, takes some concentration. Turnings are always transitions, calling for adjustment. If one of us falls out of step, he or she needs to take a double step, a skip-step, to get back into rhythm. This requires a second or two of intensified concentration. Once back in step, we're fine.

Imagine with me this scenario: A certain couple seems content with the even rhythm of their life together. Then one day, one of them becomes interested in some new venture, an exercise or sport activity, a community project, or an academic course of study. To the other spouse, the change in her or his activity pattern arrives like an uninvited guest.

He or she may think, "I don't understand. What was wrong with the way things were?" The new activity may appear like an intruder wedging into the closeness of their marriage. But for the one trying on the new interest, his or her mate may seem stubborn and unyielding: "Why don't you try some new, refreshing activity yourself? Then we can both grow."

When considering the invitation to become active, the non-adventuring one may think, "I feel exhausted just thinking about it! Take on a new activity on top of all I'm already doing? It's impossible." He or she feels that a huge demand has been made, requiring a great output of energy. For what?

The two are out of step with each other's rhythm. Although the issue seems to have appeared out of nowhere, the other doesn't feel that way. She or he has been thinking about it for a long time, though perhaps unconsciously.

Let's apply: Before considering how to get back in step with each other, try this first: Focus on being in step with the Holy Spirit, who has always been the source of spiritual energy for each of us: "Since we live by the Spirit, let us keep in step with the Spirit" (Galatians 5:25, NIV). Listen for one idea, truth, or perspective from God's Word that interests you, making you come alive. Within 24 hours, act upon one part, if only a small one.

Let's pray together: Lord God, please grant us an extra measure of patience. We look first to you, that we might become more aligned with you and your will. We commend ourselves as a couple to your love and leadership. We want to live within range of your expressed will. "Since we live by the Spirit, let us keep in step with the Spirit." Amen.

CHAPTER 63

IN STEP, IN SYNCH-II

If we are living now by the Holy Spirit, let us follow the Holy Spirit's leading in every part of our lives.

—Galatians 5:25

Today in midwinter Minnesota the windchill is 25 below. Surprise—Julie and I walked indoors this morning, on a walking track surrounding a soccer field.

We walk in step with each other. Previously I mentioned that sometimes when we make 90 degree turns, we may get out of step, necessitating an extra skip-step to get back into cadence with each other. In taking the skip-step, I am not always swan-smooth. At first I was a little self-conscious being observed that way. Then one day I decided to trash the fear.

Between married couples, sometimes one or the other may slip out of their usual daily rhythm and try a new venture. One partner may feel left behind. She or he may think others are noticing more than they actually are.

Let me encourage you: act as if you aren't even aware they're watching. Make your necessary adjustments. If someone asks why you two aren't both doing the same activities you once were, take the high road. Practice *noblesse oblige*, benignly neglecting to acknowledge your friends' lack of taste in not keeping their opinions to themselves. Noblesse oblige includes the art of deciding *not* to notice *everything* people say about you. Solomon described this art in Ecclesiastes 7:21 (NIV) "Do not pay attention to every word people say, or you may hear your servant cursing you." The high road is usually the uncrowded but God-pleasing path of those who're walking in step with the Spirit. This strategy buys you time: You may opt to continue your new activity, or your spouse may choose to join you. Or he/she may consider trying some other new interest.

President Teddy Roosevelt said, "It is not the critic who counts, not the man who points out how the strong man stumbled or where the doer of the deeds could have done better. The credit belongs to the man who is actually in the arena; whose face is marred by dust and sweat and blood; who strives valiantly, who errs and comes up short again and again; . . . who spends himself in a worthy cause; who at the best knows in the end the triumph of high achievement; and who at the worst, if he fails, at least fails while daring greatly; so that his place shall never be with those cold and timid souls who know neither defeat or victory."

Let's apply: Practice affirming each other not merely for easy victories, but for those activities which involve great effort, daring initiative, steady patience, and hearty faith. If you do decide to tweak some small detail in your partner's effort, smile warmly and humbly as you mention it.

Let's pray together: Thanks, Lord, for training us to be faithful and resilient in our efforts. Help us to walk and work in close coordination with each other whenever we can. Guide us always to remember God's word through Paul: "If we are living now by the Holy Spirit, let us follow the Holy Spirit's leading in every part of our lives." Amen.

CHAPTER 64

WHOLE GRAIN WORDS

Don't use foul or abusive language. Let everything you say be good and helpful, so that your words will be an encouragement to those who hear them.

—Ephesians 4:29

Talk is cheap. But that doesn't mean it isn't powerful. Our words can pack dynamite to crumble and tear down. Or they can heal, depending on the talker's word choices, tone, gesture, facial and eye expression, smile, or frown. Words can even reverse illness quickly, like the new TPA (Tissue Plasminogen Activator) injection often administered in emergency rooms to those who've just had a heart attack or stroke. It breaks up clotted blood in minutes, healing and saving lives.

Paul wrote to the Ephesians, warmly urging them to consciously drop all toxic, unwholesome talk. Instead, he said to speak words that build people up, retooling their faith and love. First, he counsels us to listen to each other well in order to know the other's needs.

Then, Paul encourages us to be aware of the needs of those with whom we speak, then to pull out of the backpack of our vocabulary words that will add health to each other's soul. At the same time, forget the junk food of foul words. Instead, feed yourself and others with whole grain words of wisdom, reality, love, joy, hope, comfort, and encouragement.

Bring to your mind the individuals you like to be with. The next time you're with them, take mental note of the kinds of words and expressions they use. Have you noticed that a great part of your enjoyment in being with them is the stimulation of the words and phrases they use? Aim to improve your own choice of words when you talk with others, especially your spouse. Paul said something similar in Colossians 4:6 (NIV), "Let your conversation be always full of *grace,* seasoned with salt, so that you may know how to answer everyone."

One more thing: When we misspeak, God is willing to forgive. He allows us the opportunity to confess to each other: "Please forgive me. The words I used were poor counterfeits of what I meant to say. Here's my new word: . . . ." So we *are* forgiven, and we generously share our forgiveness with each other. God cares deeply for us and our relationships. He grants us new gifts to paint over errant brush strokes.

Let's apply: Write down and then read aloud to each other some of your favorite Bible verses, ones that have eased you over hurdles in the past. And share with your spouse words you've come upon in newspapers, magazines, letters, greeting cards, radio, or books. Build up each other's confidence in the power of nourishing words.

Let's pray together: Thank you for every wholesome helping of delicious words that have nourished us. Help us speak fortified whole grain words that are full of spiritual strength and nutrition. In Jesus, the Bread of Life. Amen.

CHAPTER 65

DEVOTIONS
ON THE ROAD

I long to see you again, for I remember your tears as we parted. And I will be filled with joy when we are together again.

—2 Timothy 1:4

Note: Please reread the story on page 93, in the Introduction to Part 2. There I told about the devotional practice of General and Mrs. Matthew Ridgway. While in separate countries—the General was in Korea and his wife was in Japan—they phoned each other every evening. Earlier in the evening at their separate locations they read the same page of the same book of devotions. Then they took turns praying together on the phone.

This way of having devotions together on a daily basis enabled them to avoid voids or vacuums from developing between them. Their practice provided them not only with emotional support, but also with the deepest kind of *spiritual communication*. Their communication strengthened their bond of trust and faith, as well as their love for God and each other. They filled potential voids/vacuums with healthy bond-producing communications. Thus they were enabled to continue patiently carrying out their important responsibilities during the difficult days of the Korean War.

This was not Floral Telegraph Delivery, but "sharing God's Word and faith by phone." It helped them withstand the temptations that can come to married couples when they're separated by distance.

What a great example to follow! Some of you travel on business. Others are parted for short or longer periods of time for various reasons. You can use this book for your long-distance devotions, or one of the fine one-page-a-day devotional booklets like *Portals of Prayer* or *Our Daily Bread.*

Paul wrote Timothy, "Recalling your tears, I long to see you, so that I may be filled with joy" (2 Timothy 1:4, NIV). Let's develop a regular pattern of receiving spiritual nourishment from God's Word, and then sharing it with our spouse—no matter where we are, no matter how busy we are. It is the best antidote for maintaining healthy married life, long distance style.

Let's apply: Ask God's help in having regular family devotions whether you're at home each night or away on business.

Let's pray together: We understand that absence can make our hearts grow fonder. It can also stretch the limits of our love. Help us develop devotional habits that work well for us, to strengthen us and our relationships both with you, O Lord, and each other. Amen.

CHAPTER 66

THINK BIG, PRAY BIGGER

Now glory be to God! By his mighty power at work within us, he is able to accomplish infinitely more than we would ever dare to ask or hope. May he be given glory in the church and in Christ Jesus forever and ever.

—Ephesians 3:20–21

"You can be anything you want to be" is the ego-appealing refrain we often hear in graduation speeches. It is important that we encourage our young people with visions of open doors of service and vocational opportunity.

But they would be better served if we encouraged them the way James did in his epistle: "Look here, you people who say, 'Today or tomorrow we are going to a certain town and will stay there a year. We will do business there and make a profit.' How do you know what will happen tomorrow . . . . What you ought to say is 'If the Lord wants me to, I will live and do this or that.'" (4:13–15).

As a couple, we place ourselves in God's capable and loving hands. We know that God wants us to succeed in marriage—he wants it even more than we do. Each time we read the passage above, God's Holy Spirit fuels our hopes that he "is able to accomplish infinitely more than we would ever dare to ask or hope."

There is a difference between praying for material blessings and for spiritual blessings. Regarding the first kind of prayer, Mother Teresa liked to pray "*according to* your will, O God" instead of "*if it is* your will, O God." It might seem like only a subtle difference in expression, but "according to your will" implies more confidence in God's desire and ability to help us, and less "iffy," as if the answer to our prayer might only *possibly* be God's will. The latter expression seems to leave the door to doubt open just a crack.

But when it comes to spiritual blessings, we don't even need to pray "according to your will, O God" because we already know that God wants to give us spiritual blessings. He says so over and over in Scripture. Whenever we pray for our needs, it's fine to think big. It's even better to PRAY BIGGER.

Let's apply: Discuss and decide on one spiritual blessing and one material blessing for which you'd like to pray.

Let's pray together: Holy Spirit of God, we bring all our needs to you. First, we bring our spiritual needs for: _____

_____

_____.

Then we bring our material needs: _____

_____

_____.

We pray this second prayer "according to your will, O God." We want to be "filled with the fullness of life and power that comes from God" (Ephesians 3:19). We pray in Jesus' gracious name. Amen.

CHAPTER 67

THE FOUNDATION

OF YOUR BEAUTY

A devotion written especially for women

Charm is deceptive, and beauty does not last; but a woman who fears the Lord will be greatly praised.

—Proverbs 31:30

One day I had an appointment with my doctor for a physical exam. After the nurse had drawn blood and we were waiting for the results, the doctor made a remark about the healthy tone of my face. I thanked him, and then he said, "One of the first things they taught us in medical school to examine—and then write on our patients' charts—is the *health tone* of their faces." He went on to explain that a lot of clues can be gleaned about a person's health from looking at his or her face.

"Beauty is in the eyes of the beholder," the adage goes. But prior to that, the state of a person's inner health is a more determining factor in producing beauty in a woman, handsomeness in a man. It all starts in her or his spirit. Do faith, joy, love, hope, and confidence reside in your heart? Those gifts and attributes directly affect your health and appearance. The converse is also true of bitterness, resentment, fear, and regret. Either can take up squatters' rights in your soul.

The fear mentioned in the passage above is not negative; it's a synonym for healthy faith and reverent trust in God. The inspired writer of Proverbs claimed that respectful trust in God is of higher value than mere physical beauty and charm. A sincere, deep love for God is always escorted by respectful awe toward God. A woman who fears, trusts, and loves the Lord, cares more about what God thinks of her than people's opinions, including her own. The woman in whose heart faith and love toward God burn brightly, cannot contain that warm light inside, but will reveal that light in the health and beauty of her face.

True beauty is not what appears on our surface. Peter describes real beauty vs. counterfeit: "Don't be concerned about the outward beauty that depends on fancy hairstyles, expensive jewelry, or beautiful clothes. You should be known for the beauty that comes from within, the unfading beauty of a gentle and quiet spirit, which is so precious to God" (1 Peter 3:3–4). It is this composure and confidence that are so appealing. They are the foundation of a woman's beauty.

Let's apply: As a married couple, you strongly influence the tone of your spouse's health, as well as your own. The condition of your health, in turn, directly affects your appearance. Assess what you can do to enhance your own and each other's health:

Wives, what can you do to enhance *your own* health? _____
_____.
_____ Your husband's health? _____
_____.

Let's pray together: Dear Lord, you give us your sustaining strength, your nourishing love, and the hope that grows from your promises. Thus you create and maintain our health and wellness. Help us to avoid health-debilitating substances, practices, and attitudes, but rather to hold fast to health-inducing ones that you prize and freely give us. In your Son's loving and holy name we pray. Amen.

CHAPTER 68

SERVING THE FAMILY, LEADING WELL

A devotion written especially for husbands/fathers

For even I, the Son of Man, came here not to be served, but to serve,
and to give my life as a ransom for many.
—Matthew 20:28

One day a Christian husband and father was reflecting on what he heard from the Bible about his role as spiritual leader: "What is my role all about? How can I tell if I'm living out my role faithfully and effectively?" Doctors are faithful and effective when they give their patients the best possible treatment, teaching and encouraging them in good health practices.

The question is: are your wife and children spiritually healthy? Do they have joy as they grow in Christ? If so, you're probably serving and leading them well in Christ.

A couple of thousand yards from our house is a growing field belonging to a major wholesale nursery company, one of the largest in the world. I look out from our second floor bay window and see one of their "Container Fields." Plants are grown there in container pots, which are inserted into the ground. The plants-in-containers are grown outdoors so they can receive sunlight and rain directly from God's sky. This method is more effective and less expensive than if they were grown inside a greenhouse. And when it comes time to sell the plants, the plastic containers can be easily pulled from the ground and shipped as they are, rather than the plants being dug up, which is more traumatic for the plant.

You husbands and fathers are like those container pots. They are simple black plastic pots, costing very little. But what they *contain*, that's the thing: live, healthy, growing plants! Similarly, your important role is to protect and enhance the spiritual health of the family members God has entrusted to you, your precious wife and children.

In the context of the passage above, Jesus contrasts government officials with himself. He says that unbelieving government leaders lord it over people, trying to gain power for themselves, rather than using their authority to benefit those they govern. In stark contrast, Jesus describes himself as the one who serves people. He said that if you want to become *great* like him, then become a servant like him. What does a *servant* do? Wait to be served? No, Jesus says. He himself did not come to be served, but to serve people by giving himself for them.

St. Paul described his significant life-changing experience in Galatians 2:20: "I have been crucified with Christ. I myself no longer live, but Christ lives in me. So I live my life in this earthly body by trusting in the Son of God who loved me and gave himself for me."

Let's apply: Husbands, fathers, mention specific tasks you fulfill in your family for the benefit of your wife and children. How do you see your actions as direct outgrowths of your faithful role as a servant-leader? In all you do, do you lead your family well by serving the cause of Christ and glorifying God?

Let's pray together: [Aloud, by husbands/fathers:] Dear Lord Jesus, I clearly hear your words, words with which you nourish and inspire me to lead by serving my family well. Dear Lord, guide me to be the best husband/father I can be, empowered and inspired by you, my only Savior and King. Amen.

CHAPTER 69

THE DAY INFATUATION GREW TO LOVE

Love is . . . not rude. Love does not demand its own way.
—1 Corinthians 13:5

On an Internet Web site called "cyberparent" I found these words describing infatuation:

"Infatuation is instant desire. It is one set of glands calling to another . . . . Infatuation is marked by a feeling of insecurity. There are nagging doubts, unanswered questions, little bits and places about your beloved that you would just as soon not examine too closely. It might spoil the dream."

By contrast, love acts differently:

"Love is quiet understanding and the mature acceptance of imperfection. It is real. It gives strength and grows beyond you to bolster your beloved . . . . Love means trust. You are calm, secure, unthreatened. Your beloved feels that and that makes them even more trustworthy."

If infatuation has a controlling hand in our behavior, it's a breeding ground for becoming self-centered and rude. We tend to think of rudeness as a result of mean-spiritedness. But when it shows up in relationships between men and women, it can be the result of infatuation that has turned sulky. When you see someone acting rudely, you may suspect that his or her anger is a cover-up for immaturity.

It's interesting that though St. Paul never married, he surely knew about love: "Love is patient and kind. Love is not jealous or boastful or proud or rude. Love does not demand its own way. Love is not irritable, and it keeps no record of when it has been wronged. . . . Love never gives up, never loses faith, is always hopeful, and endures through every circumstance" (1 Corinthians 13:4–7). Love between married people grows as each learns new and exciting truths about the other ("love rejoices when the truth wins out"). Loving another person makes life together exciting and filled with hope.

I don't remember when Julie's and my relationship grew from infatuation into love, but it did—not that we've finished growing.

Let's apply: If you have teenage children, practice explaining to them the difference between infatuation and love. Notice how your own understanding deepens in the telling.

Let's pray together: Lord, we know that you want us to grow in maturity. We admit that we're not completely there yet. Grant us your forgiveness and guidance so that our infatuation continually ripens into love that builds up our spouse—which is what you plan to happen. Amen.

CHAPTER 70

DON'T LET GRACE
LEAVE YOUR MARRIAGE-I

Learning from our divorced brothers and sisters

Be considerate as you live with (each other), and treat (your spouse) with respect . . . as an heir with you of the gracious gift of life, so that nothing will hinder your prayers.

—1 Peter 3:7 (NIV)

We can learn a great deal from couples who have been divorced.

It all started when the husband and I had lunch together. As we were saying goodbye, he said, "You know, when grace leaves a marriage . . . ." A couple of days later I asked if I could interview him and his new wife.

When we sat down in their family room, they spoke of their former marriages. Picking up on the expression he had used in the restaurant "when grace leaves a marriage," he explained further: "If you don't watch out and deal with daily issues, they build up. And then it's too long a row to hoe to get back to graciousness."

I couldn't help but think about the passage above from 1 Peter, about married couples being "heirs together of the gracious gift of life." If we are not considerate and treat each other with respect, obstacles may form that "hinder our prayers."

The husband traced the next step in the weakening of his and his former wife's marriage: "I just began to feel hopeless. I started thinking: 'It's not worth it. There's no forgiveness here anymore. I won't be appreciated, no matter what I do. Even if I keep trying, I'll never measure up.'" He added, "I don't mean that we couldn't have expectations toward each other anymore, but all we had left was the measuring stick by which we judged each other."

Afterward, I thought to myself, "I hope and pray that grace never leaves my marriage." And then, recalling what he had said about the measuring stick, I realized that in God's sight I definitely do not measure up. Nor does my wife, nor does any of us. We can all judge and find ourselves—and one another—wanting. The good news is that God understands that we humans cannot dig ourselves out of the hole of guilt. That's when *he* took action. He sent his beloved Son here. He submitted to the measuring stick of God's law in our place, though he had done nothing wrong. He let himself receive the sentence of death, so that we could receive the gift of life, grace, and forgiveness. He pulled us out of the pit.

Let's apply: As you discuss this devotion, try to recall a time when you felt judged by your partner. And then the situation changed somehow and you no longer felt accused. What accounted for the change? Each of you, come up with one example.

Let's pray together: Dear Father, we realize that neither of us is without fault. We know you provide enough forgiveness for both our own and our partner's shortcomings. Please never let grace leave our marriage. In our Savior's loving name. Amen.

CHAPTER 71

DON'T LET GRACE
LEAVE YOUR MARRIAGE-II

Learning from our divorced brothers and sisters

Be considerate as you live with (each other), and treat (your spouse)
with respect . . . as an heir with you of the gracious gift of life, so that
nothing hinders your prayers.

—1 Peter 3:7 (NIV)

The couple and I continued our discussion. The subject came up
of wives and husbands looking into each other's eyes, like when
they're driving together in a car.

The man said, "You know how you can be driving along, and you
notice her looking at you? You trade glances. I noticed grace was leaving our marriage when we could no longer look into each other's eyes
for very long. I began to ask myself, 'Can I look into her eyes without
looking away?' and realized that I could no longer do that."

He expanded on that, posing a generalized question, "Do she (his
new wife) and I look at each other as gifts from God? If not, then we
are just looking at each other the way the world does. And then we get
back to the measuring stick idea, where we assess each other on the basis
of our selfish desires and what we want from that person."

This time his wife picked up the conversational thread and said, "I
find now that I'm praying for my husband differently than I did in my

first marriage. Now I pray first for him as a person. Then I pray for his real needs and the desires of his heart. Following that, I pray for God to show me what steps I can take to help fill his needs."

When we began the conversation, the couple had been sitting on opposite ends of the couch, with the center cushion empty between them. As the woman talked about her love for her husband and her newfound prayer life, the center cushion was no longer empty. They filled it with the intertwined fingers of their hands. It was a slam dunk to go from the three of us talking about each other, to our praying directly to God. I blessed them, asking our heavenly Father to protect them and sustain his invaluable grace in their union. Then they prayed for each other. It was a holy moment.

Let's apply: Be brave. Flip a coin to determine which of you will start. Answer this question: "My wife's (husband's) two or three real needs *at this time* are: _____, _____ _____, and _____. Then propose some specific actions *you* can do to help fill his or her needs. You'll no doubt receive some helpful input from your partner.

Let's pray together: Please stimulate once again our appreciation of the grace with which you've adorned our lives. Thank you for granting us the huge blessing of being married to each other. May we allow nothing—neither a problem we're grappling with nor a success we're pleased with—to dilute our gratefulness to you. The love that comes from your generous heart is what created and sustains our love for each other. We pray in the name of our dear Lord Jesus. Amen.

CHAPTER 72

"RESPECTFULLY YOURS . . ."

Show respect for everyone.

—1 Peter 2:17

Give respect and honor to all to whom it is due.

—Romans 13:7

A kindhearted woman gains respect.

—Proverbs 11:16 (NIV)

Teach older men to exercise self-control, to be worthy of respect, and to live wisely.

—Titus 2:2

Near the end of my father's life, he mentioned to me that he and my mother had the long-standing habit of holding a "heart to heart" about once every three months. During those times they would discuss issues, air out problems, and release accumulated feelings.

Though Julie's and my "heart to hearts" aren't as frequent as my parents', she and I try to discuss our issues in that same spirit of respect. Though some may think of showing respect as a passive action, it is really quite active and intentional because it is fueled by a sense of hope.

As I visualize my parents having their "heart to hearts," I see the loving, patient respect they held for each other. Their mutual love gave them the courage to be honest with each other.

A healthy relationship with God—please, Holy Spirit, may ours always be so—is built on faith and respect. Respect and love for God bears the wonderful fruit of respect for other persons, especially our wives and husbands.

Respecting, trusting, and loving God builds into our personality the capacity to respect people. Admiring and appreciating God and all he has done, builds into our spirit good, healthy self-esteem. Then self-esteem gives birth to prizing and respecting people.

When we respect people, we have a sense of hope toward them. From those whom we respect, we expect great things—not just to get something for ourselves, or satisfy some selfish desire. Rather, we have a sense of high expectation about what they will accomplish. We say in effect, "You can do this, I know in my heart you can." Our partner picks up on our healthy expectation based on our high respect for them. And that in turn stimulates their self-confidence.

Numerous studies have been done in classrooms, analyzing the effect of teachers showing a sense of confidence and high expectation toward their students. If that is true in the relationship between teachers and students, how much more powerfully does this chemistry work between wives and husbands, who love and respect each other.

Let's apply: During a few minutes of perhaps unexpected quiet time—like waiting in your doctor's office—write on a slip of paper a few of your spouse's good attributes. After each one, add a phrase prayer such as, "Thank you, Lord, for giving him/her these traits of _____ and _____."

Let's pray together: Gracious heavenly Father, help us unselfishly acknowledge each other's gifts and positive personality traits. Help us reflect on all the goodness you have invested in my husband/wife. Aid us to grow further in our desire and ability to show sincere respect and admiration for each other. In Jesus, our Brother. Amen.

CHAPTER 73

PERMISSION ASKED

AND GRANTED

Keep on asking, and you will be given what you ask for.
—Matthew 7:7

I believe in this important prerequisite for fruitful discussion: when there is a matter of substance you feel a need to take up, ask for permission to talk. Begin with words like: "There is something I'd like to talk over and get your opinion, Honey. Would now be a good time, or would later be better?"

My wife Julie worked in human resources at the 3M Company in St. Paul, Minnesota. One day she was invited to a management seminar led by a consultant from outside the company.

The speaker made this observation: "When we relate to those in our department, we often treat them like dirt. We tend to make assumptions and demands, for example, regarding deadlines." Instead, he strongly asserted, "Let's treat coworkers as if they were *clients,* with the same respect and courtesy we would show someone whose business we want."

Sounds revolutionary, doesn't it? There is a similar dynamic in our relationships as husbands and wives. Asking our spouse for permission when we want to discuss a matter of importance allows our partner time to prepare him- or herself emotionally. If he or she isn't too busy or tired, the time might be that very moment. Otherwise the two of you can set up another time when you can be at your best.

Respectfully asking for and receiving permission to talk about important matters is appropriate for a couple who've been joined in marriage by their heavenly Father. Try this and watch your success rate in problem-solving rise significantly.

Let's apply: As you can see, the application is already built into this devotion. Ask permission for "a time to talk," either right now (if both of you are relatively rested and not too busy) or at another time in the next day or two. In your mind, envision the good outcome: You are relaxed and at your best. With love and carefulness you talk things over. You arrive at a workable solution in the short term, and you share some ideas about matters for the longer term. If it works out well, analyze why. If not, analyze why the method didn't work this time. Then in a few days, try this method again.

Let's pray together: Gracious Lord Jesus, thank you for the opportunity to practice this orderly way to discuss and deal successfully with our issues and projects. In your mercy, calm our hearts and clear our minds. Assure us of your constant love, forgiveness, and guidance as we grow, partnering with you and each other. Thank you for designating us as "heirs together of the gracious gift of life" (1 Peter 3:7, NIV). Thanks for each small success you grant us, every one a gift of your grace and favor. Amen.

To order additional copies of

DEVOTED TO
GOD
a *n* *d*
EACH OTHER

Have your credit card ready and call

Toll free: (877) 421-READ (7323)

or order online at: www.winepressbooks.com

Thanksgiving Log

**Events in which God's provision and/
or intervention significantly helped us.**

(Include not only present but also past events even from your childhood.)

"The Lord our God is near us whenever we pray to him . . . . Only
be careful …that you do not forget the things your eyes have seen or
let them slip from your heart as long as you live. Teach them to your
children and to their children after them."
                                                    —Deuteronomy 4:7 & 9, NIV

Date   Event

_____   _____

_____   _____

_____   _____

_____   _____

_____   _____

_____   _____

_____   _____

_____   _____

_____   _____

THANKSGIVING LOG

**Events in which God's provision and/
or intervention significantly helped us.**
(Include not only present but also past events even from your childhood.)

"The Lord our God is near us whenever we pray to him . . . . Only
be careful …that you do not forget the things your eyes have seen or
let them slip from your heart as long as you live. Teach them to your
children and to their children after them."
—Deuteronomy 4:7 & 9, NIV

Date   Event

_____   _____

_____   _____

_____   _____

_____   _____

_____   _____

_____   _____

_____   _____

_____   _____

THANKSGIVING LOG

**Events in which God's provision and/
or intervention significantly helped us.**

(Include not only present but also past events even from your childhood.)

"The Lord our God is near us whenever we pray to him . . . . Only be careful ...that you do not forget the things your eyes have seen or let them slip from your heart as long as you live. Teach them to your children and to their children after them."
—Deuteronomy 4:7 & 9, NIV

Date   Event

_____   _____

_____   _____

_____   _____

_____   _____

_____   _____

_____   _____

_____   _____

_____   _____

_____   _____

JOURNAL

JOURNAL

JOURNAL

Journal

JOURNAL

_____

_____

_____

_____

_____

_____

_____

_____

_____

_____

_____

_____

_____

_____

_____

_____

_____

_____

JOURNAL

_____

_____

_____

_____

_____

_____

_____

_____

_____

_____

_____

_____

_____

_____

_____

_____

_____

JOURNAL

_____

_____

_____

_____

_____

_____

_____

_____

_____

_____

_____

_____

_____

_____

_____

_____

_____

_____

JOURNAL

JOURNAL

JOURNAL

Journal

JOURNAL

_____

_____

_____

_____

_____

_____

_____

_____

_____

_____

_____

_____

_____

_____

_____

_____

_____

_____

JOURNAL

Journal

JOURNAL

Journal

JOURNAL

_____

_____

_____

_____

_____

_____

_____

_____

_____

_____

_____

_____

_____

_____

_____

_____

_____

_____

JOURNAL